MW01038680

Praise for *The OPA! Way*

"'Meaning is being,' said the great philosopher-physicist David Bohm. The flip side of this nugget of wisdom is that without positive meaning our life is empty, dull, and a drain on those around us. *The OPA! Way* is a meaning-filled alternative, a doorway to a fulfilling, majestic, and joy-filled existence, seen through the prism of perennial Greek insight."

—LARRY DOSSEY, MD, author, *One Mind: How Our Individual Mind Is Part of a Greater Consciousness and Why It Matters*

"At a time when the world seems to be plunging ahead into a future dominated by information technology, apps, increasing individual isolation in a cyber-environment, and obsessive preoccupation with answering one's emails, *The OPA! Way* offers something else: a life based on values that go back to ancient Greece; a world in which friends and neighbors spend time together exchanging ideas and experiences; and a future in which service to others offers the richest personal rewards. Is there any doubt that *The OPA! Way* is by far the better path?"

—MICHAEL S. DUKAKIS, former Massachusetts governor and U.S. presidential nominee; distinguished professor of political science

"For me, *The OPA! Way* is the ONLY way. This is not just a book. This is a profound, soul-enriching philosophy that captures the true meaning and essence of our lives. *The OPA! Way* is guaranteed to change the way you see the world forever. I recommend everyone read this book."

—DEBBIE MATENOPOULOS, author of the best-selling cookbook *It's All Greek to Me* and two-time Emmy Award nominee

"Having reviewed several recent books on meaning in life, I finally found a book that really addresses the fundamental issue of human existence in a lucid and practical manner—*The OPA! Way*. Inspired by Odysseus and informed by Viktor Frankl, the authors are able to show us the profound truth that meaningfulness lies in connecting with meaningful relationships, deeper purpose, and an appreciative attitude. Alex Pattakos and Elaine Dundon have just written another bestseller!"

—DR. PAUL T. P. WONG, editor of
The Human Quest for Meaning, 2nd edition

"A must-read and good parenting, teaching, or self-help tool, as the daily affirmations of *The OPA! Way* are time-tested methods on how to live the good life and 'enjoy yourself' in the pursuit of happiness in a way that honors and best serves the well-being of individuals, communities, and, in turn, all of humanity."

—GEORGE ELIAS STEPHANOPOULOS, executive producer
of *Golf in the Kingdom* and creator of the film *Swing Away*
set in Crete, Greece

"This is an extraordinary book with many insights and directions for leading a healthier, happier, and more meaningful life. Congratulations to Alex Pattakos and Elaine Dundon for your exceptional contribution to Living."

—E. MIKE VASILOMANOLAKIS, MD, chief of staff and director,
cardiology division, Community Hospital of Long Beach,
California; Grammy Award–winning music producer

"Alex Pattakos and Elaine Dundon have done it again. With *The OPA! Way*, they brilliantly articulate that we all need meaningful relationships, must engage with deeper purpose, and must tackle life with the goal that we can truly make a difference. This book is indeed a prescription for lives worth living for all of us!"

—THE HONOURABLE CAROLYN BENNETT, MD, member of
Parliament (Canada)

"Truly . . . outstanding! I can't begin to tell you how this book touched my heart, spirit, mind, and body. I believe *The OPA! Way* should be mandatory reading for everyone! It should be taught in schools. Doctors, psychologists, nutritionists, employers, coaches, athletes, fathers, mothers, presidents, and all people around the world should have this on a special bookshelf and incorporate it into their lives and work. At the tender age of 18 months old, I became a type 1 diabetic. I have no recollection of any life other than a daily routine of checking my blood sugars and taking insulin shots. Life for me is always a bit tenuous. Yet, I am so blessed to be a diabetic for no other reason than it has made me understand what is truly important on this journey of life. It's all here in this inspirational book, as Alex and Elaine take you on a beautiful odyssey of meaning and purpose while visiting Greece. Like Alex, my family comes from the Sfakia region of Crete. It was such a joy to read about the Cretan people and Greek people in general and the beauty they carry naturally within. They are grateful for the simplest things in life. We all should be grateful. The world has much to offer us . . . and us to it. Thank you, Alex and Elaine. I feel our souls are one. Okay, I am ready to dance and take off on my journey again . . . OPA!"

—ADONI MAROPIS, actor, filmmaker, and athlete

"Alex and Elaine have made profound connections between the wisdom of the ancient Greeks and the crises of modern life to help us all chart a path toward a life of meaning."

—JOHN METAXAS, news anchor, CBS New York

"Until *The OPA! Way*, the benefits of growing up within the community-oriented and human-centered Greek culture were buried way back in the depths of my childhood mind. Greeks have always lived in symbiotic harmony between individual ambition and the common good, called the 'village.' As the son of Greek immigrants and growing up in Chicago's close-knit Greek community, this was second nature to me, and something I took for granted. OPA! Alex and Elaine, thank you for reminding me!"

—JOHN P. CALAMOS, SR., founder, chairman, CEO, Co-CIO, Calamos Asset Management, Inc.

"'OPA!,' a well-known exclamation deciphered into the core of human existence and existential sanity. With insight, sensitivity, and knowledge, Alex Pattakos and Elaine Dundon go beyond scientific or philosophical observations and ascertainments. In simple words and examples they present the core philosophy for a meaningful life, which could even be called survival in this difficult era. *The OPA! Way*, based on ancient tried values of humanity, forgotten in the antagonistic quest for progress and power through the years, proposes a practical and feasible answer to the eternal question of dealing with life with a reason for living, through dignity and respect for oneself and the people around. A must-read book for every thinking human being, and its content especially discussed with the younger generation of today!"

—ALIKI MITSAKOS, MD, PHD, cofounder, The International Center for Leading Studies, Athens, Greece

"I love it. *The OPA! Way* is one of the most important books on Meaning to come along in years because it is based on the wisdom of Greek philosophers and traditional Greek culture. Breaking and going beyond the stereotypes that typically define what it means to be 'Greek,' *The OPA! Way* is a celebration of Greek life that offers a rare yet very practical guide to finding joy and meaning in everyday life. I applaud Alex and Elaine for their insights and advice that show all of us, Greeks and those not of Greek heritage, that living a life of meaning is possible. Let's all say, 'OPA!'"

—GREGORY C. PAPPAS, founder and chairman, Greek America Foundation; CEO, The Pappas Media Group; and founder and publisher, *Greek America Magazine* and *The Pappas Post*

"In a day and age when most of us have too much to do and too little time to do it, Alex and Elaine have written a book that's sorely needed. They provide ageless and wise advice on what really matters—a life worth living. I hope that you take the time to read it, study it, and most importantly, LIVE it. I know I plan to."

—FRANK YIANNAS, vice president of food safety for Global Brands, Walmart; adjunct professor, Michigan State University; past president, International Association for Food Protection; and author of *Food Safety Culture*

"In *The OPA! Way*, Alex Pattakos and Elaine Dundon turn to Greek culture as its muse for defining the meaning of life and find a treasure trove of insightful discoveries about the human spirit. After you read it, you'll want to shout 'OPA!'"

—NIKI LEONDAKIS, CEO, Commune Hotels & Resorts

"Alex and Elaine generously share with us what was so graciously shared with them on their travels through Greece: how to find the true joy of living based on very simple yet fulfilling principles. From philosophical concepts to spiritual principles to dietary suggestions, this delightful book continues to stimulate ideas long after the final page is finished. This is NOT self-help. This is help yourself . . . to a beautiful life, *The OPA! Way!*"

—DON FERTMAN, chief development officer, Subway, and founder, Recovery Branches

"Alex and Elaine capture the essence and secrets of the balanced and beautiful life passed on from the ancient world and made relevant, meaningful, and so inspiring in contemporary times. *The OPA! Way: Finding Joy & Meaning in Everyday Life & Work* is a mirror of the glory that IS Greece—embedded in each individual—just waiting to be unleashed. Alex and Elaine provide catharsis and the 'Way' through a compelling and thoroughly enjoyable treasure and page-turner. Bravo and OPA!"

—ART DIMOPOULOS, executive director, National Hellenic Society

"Alex and Elaine achieved a quite complex and challenging goal—they wrote a book on meaning by putting it in a quite unusual context: 'Hellenism vs. Globalization.' They define the meaning of life through a continuous confrontation of the values/practices of the global (American) capitalism with those of Hellenism (as it has been reflected in the ancient fables and the modern Cretan/Greek villages' way of living). They present in a simple and clear way the imbalances and the causes for personal and social catastrophes or disasters by contrasti~g turbo capitalism to an 'anthrocapitalism,' the essence of which is *The OPA! Way* of thinking and acting. Hellenism can formulate a future and hope to humanity for years to come."

—PANAGIOTIS KARKATSOULIS, PHD, founder, Institute for Regulatory Policy Research; policy advisor, Hellenic Ministry of Administrative Reform and eGovernment; and professor, National School of Public Administration, Athens, Greece

"Alex and Elaine addressed a huge number of important and complex issues. Each reader will find something in *The OPA! Way* that will enrich his or her inner world. I warmly recommend the reading of *The OPA! Way*, preferably in the plane that will take you to Greece or under the warm sun and clean skies of the blue and white country."

—DR. ANGELOS PANGRATIS, ambassador of the European Union to the World Trade Organization, Geneva, Switzerland

"Who would have thought that three little letters (O-P-A!) together would make such a BIG word. *The OPA! Way* is truly a life-changing read that infuses a Hellenic flavor of purpose and meaning in all we are and do . . . thank you, Alex and Elaine, for this inspiring work!"

—STEVE AGI, publisher and managing editor,
OPA! Magazine, Australia

"While reading *The OPA! Way: Finding Joy & Meaning in Everyday Life & Work*, I yearned to dance like Zorba and change my last name to 'Kampmannzakis.' But Alex and Elaine brilliantly show how *The OPA! Way* principles of meaningful and purposeful connection to both ourselves and to others flow within each of us no matter who we are, no matter where we live (although I still dream to dance like Zorba on a beach in Crete!)."

—STEVEN KAMPMANN, writer, director, and educator

"*The OPA! Way* provides a meaningful pathway for helping to rebrand Greece and rediscover the true Greek spirit. Alex and Elaine also inspire and guide us to look for meaning in our everyday lives. This is a must read book. OPA!"

—AGAPI STASSINOPOULOS, author, *Unbinding the Heart: A Dose of Greek Wisdom, Generosity, and Unconditional Love*

"Aside from being a wonderfully entertaining and fun read, this book is educational and an inspirational way to find true meaning in Life. Simply said, it's the perfect and complete guide for a better and happier life in general."

—DIRK DALICHAU, lifestyle hotelier, chief operating officer, Ovolo Group, Hong Kong

"Kudos to authors Pattakos and Dundon for their inspiring look at how we can introduce meaning into our personal and business lives. Their unique approach of using the words of the ancient Greek philosophers in conjunction with the words and lives of current day Greek citizens results in an effective form of storytelling. One that provides a template upon which they can examine the micro as well as the macro effects of living a life with meaning."

—KAREN BLOOM, Bloom, Gross & Associates, Chicago

"Alex and Elaine have described, in a very compelling and readable way, an approach to finding meaning that readers can apply not only in their workplaces but, more importantly, in their lives. Even if you're not of Greek heritage, the lessons in this book can help you live a fuller and more meaningful life. And, after all, that's what it's really all about—or should be."

—BOB LAVIGNA, assistant vice chancellor, human resources, University of Wisconsin; author, *Engaging Government Employees*

The
OPA!
Way

The
OPA!
Way

Finding Joy & Meaning

in Everyday Life & Work

ALEX PATTAKOS and
ELAINE DUNDON

BenBella Books, Inc.
Dallas, TX

This book is for informational purposes only. It is not intended to serve as a substitute for professional medical advice. The authors and publisher specifically disclaim any and all liability arising directly or indirectly from the use of any information contained in this book. A health care professional should be consulted regarding your specific medical situation. Any product mentioned in this book does not imply endorsement of that product by the authors or publisher.

Copyright © 2015 by Alex Pattakos and Elaine Dundon

All rights reserved. No part of this book may be used or reproduced in any manner whatsoever without written permission except in the case of brief quotations embodied in critical articles or reviews.

BenBella Books, Inc.
10300 N. Central Expressway, Suite #530 | Dallas, TX 75231
www.benbellabooks.com | Send feedback to feedback@benbellabooks.com

Printed in the United States of America
10 9 8 7 6 5 4 3 2 1

Library of Congress Cataloging-in-Publication Data
Pattakos, Alex.
 The OPA! way : finding joy & meaning in everyday life & work / Alex Pattakos & Elaine Dundon.
  pages cm
 Includes bibliographical references and index.
 ISBN 978-1-940363-25-7 (trade cloth : alkaline paper)—ISBN 978-1-940363-51-6 (electronic) 1. Greece—Social life and customs. 2. Greeks—Psychology. 3. Philosophy, Ancient. 4. Conduct of life. 5. Social values. 6. Self-actualization (Psychology) I. Dundon, Elaine, 1959- II. Title.
 DF741.P395 2014
 650.1—dc23
                                    2014018819

Editing by Heather Butterfield | Copyediting by Francesa Drago
Proofreading by Greg Tegaue and Rainbow Graphics
Graphic design by W. Scott Matthews
Cover design by Bradford Foltz | Jacket design by Sarah Dombrowsky
Text design and composition by Silver Feather Design
Printed by Lake Book Manufacturing

Distributed by Perseus Distribution | www.perseusdistribution.com
To place orders through Perseus Distribution: Tel: (800) 343-4499
Fax: (800) 351-5073 | E-mail: orderentry@perseusbooks.com

Significant discounts for bulk sales are available. Please contact
Glenn Yeffeth at glenn@benbellabooks.com or (214) 750-3628.

*Dedicated to the ancient Greek philosophers
and traditional Greek villagers
who taught us so much about how to live the good life,
as well as to all the people around the world
who are searching for meaning.*

Contents

PART FIVE
The Odyssey Continues . . .

Part One

Introduction

1

OPA! Our Odyssey

THE SUN WAS SHINING AND the sky appeared bluer than usual. We could even see our reflections in the crystal-clear water of the Cretan Sea as it gently kissed the shoreline much like it must have done when Odysseus, the legendary Greek king of Ithaka and hero of Homer's epic poem *The Odyssey*, passed by the same spot thousands of years before. It is Odysseus and, of course, Homer, whom we must thank for giving us the popular word "odyssey" and its deeper meaning, which is now associated with the idea of traveling along life's uncharted path. And like Odysseus, we view life as an odyssey into the unexpected, as well as an adventure to be embraced and experienced to the fullest.

It would not be too far-fetched to say that it was the spirit of Odysseus that guided us along the path toward writing this book. The idea behind and catalyst for the book, which not only sent us off on our journey to Greece but also helped to chart its direction, came from the existential question people kept asking us over the years, "How can we live more meaningful lives?" As leaders, professors, consultants, and personal mentors, no matter what the task or subject matter in which we were involved, the need, not simply the desire, to be engaged in a meaningful life and with meaningful work, would surface. We observed that there is a basic human need to be engaged in meaningful relationships with others—family, friends, neighbors, co-workers, even acquaintances—and to feel that life has a purpose, that it really matters. More often than not, we found that it was the search for meaning that motivated and sustained people through both good and not-so-good times.

As we wondered why the search for meaning was becoming such an important and pervasive topic, it seemed only natural for us to go on an exploration, like our Greek ancestor Odysseus, in search of an answer.

However, we discovered from the start that finding an answer would be much easier said than done. Setting sail into the abyss was one thing; charting a course that would bring us to our intended destination was quite another since no maps were readily available to guide us along the way. Again, like the explorer Odysseus, we had to rely not only on our knowledge and past experience, but also on our deeper sense of inner "knowing" or intuition. Sure, many people over the ages had searched for and written about the same existential question that triggered our quest. Like sponges recovered by divers from the waters around the Greek islands, we soaked up as much of this existing information as possible. We spoke with thousands of people who sought meaning in their lives but we still weren't finding the answers to what makes life meaningful. Instead, we found more insight into the issues facing people in these challenging times.

The Lack of Meaning

We encountered many people who told us that they felt that "something was missing." They told us they were feeling overwhelmed, lonely, and unfulfilled in their personal lives. They told us they were stressed in the workplace, unsure of how they fit with their group or organization's overall purpose, and irritated by their coworkers' lack of empathy and trust. Generally, they felt disconnected and not fully engaged. Retired people shared with us that they had lost their way, and perhaps even their sense of identity and self-worth, without the structure of work and the social connections that work brings. Students shared with us that the stresses of achieving in school and understanding the fast-paced, complex world were too much for them.

A pessimistic air seems to have engulfed our world, with increased levels of stress due to unemployment, financial hardship, and health and relationship issues. People express the meaninglessness of their lives through addictions—to television, sex, food, alcohol, drugs, shopping, gambling, the internet, etc. Depression and anxiety are on the rise, leading to record numbers of prescriptions being written for antidepressants. Impatience and aggression are also on the rise, as more and more people believe their individual needs are more important than those of others or society's as a whole. Today we see that despite being in an increasingly networked and connected world, too many people feel disconnected and untrusting—of neighbors, coworkers, leaders of organizations and, especially, of government.

Despite being able to choose amongst so many consumer goods, people are actually feeling overwhelmed with all the choices that are available. Unfortunately, society has told us that we can achieve happiness through consumption. Society has made us think *if only* . . . "If only I had a bigger house, a better car, more money, and a better job, I would be fulfilled." But more choices and personal freedoms have led to higher expectations, which in turn have led to never being satisfied with what we have! We think we want more, but when we get it, it is not enough. We still want more. "Enough" becomes a moving target. And we spend so much time working to pay for things we don't really want, let alone need. In the pursuit of the "if only," we have sacrificed our relationships, our health, and our sanity.

We've also been taught that we should expect to have it all and we should expect to have it *now*. In other words, we are driven by instant gratification—and justify it with thoughts like *just put it on credit, there's no need to earn the money today*, and *pay for it later*. Not just individuals but cities, states, and nations have embraced these beliefs. So is it any real shock that, one day this way of thinking would be challenged by the consequences, including unsustainable debt? As this global issue unfolds, accelerates, and intensifies, and the stark reality of the economic crisis sinks in, is there any reason to wonder why more and more people are asking seriously about the meaning of life?

Even the relentless pursuit of pleasure and power has shown itself to be short-lived because pleasure and power are founded on the same "if only I had more" logic. Left unchecked, these pursuits comprise a vicious cycle and manifest themselves as an endless—and joyless—undertaking, much like the one experienced by the Greek hero Sisyphus, who was ordered by the gods to push a big rock uphill only to see it slip out of his hands in the very last moment and roll down the hill once more.

There is something deeper happening in our world. The real crisis *behind* our current economic crisis is the Crisis of Meaning, which affects all aspects of our lives: We've lost the authentic connection with others. We've lost the ability to engage with the deeper purpose of our lives. We've lost the ability to embrace the fullness of life with enthusiasm, energy, and joy.

The Good News!

The good news about this Crisis of Meaning is that it has forced us to ask better questions and reassess our lives and priorities. It has forced us to ask, "How can we live more meaningful lives?" It's a question that gets us back to the core of our being—to the essence of our humanness. It's a universal question that's been asked and pondered for thousands of years. Almost twenty-five hundred years ago, the Greek philosopher Plato also considered this question and proclaimed, "Man—a being in search of meaning."

Our Backgrounds

We, too, were examining our lives and asking the same meaning-focused question. We both grew up in North America and adopted the traditional Western values of hard work and "the pursuit of happiness." We spent many years as leaders, professors, and writers in the field of innovation management, helping people in both business and public service generate ideas and plans for new initiatives based on our book, *The Seeds of Innovation*. It was interesting work but somehow, at the end of the day, we both felt that something was missing: there was too much "faster, better, cheaper"; too much chasing the "next best thing"; and too much head and not enough heart. So we began to shift to the human side of work and life with the publication of our book, *Prisoners of Our Thoughts*. Our work was successful, yet we still questioned what was really fulfilling and meaningful to us, our clients, their customers, and, importantly, society as a whole. So it only seemed natural for us to embark on our own odyssey in search of an answer . . .

The Land of Philosophers

Because Greece is the land of philosophers and since Alex just happens to come from a long line of Greeks, we felt that it would be a great place to pursue our odyssey. We traveled many times to Greece, well before its recent economic crisis

7

began, to research and experience what eventually became the new paradigm introduced in this book. We soon realized that much of what we had learned over the years had grown in importance as the country's crisis unfolded and intensified.

Greece is undergoing tremendous change right now—economically, socially, politically, and psychologically. Like other countries, Greece borrowed too much and spent too much, leading to high and unsustainable debt. This overspending, combined with a lack of oversight for public funds and also corruption and tax evasion, was a signal that the Greeks had drifted away from their traditional core values. As a small country, unable to print more money, Greece faces a challenging future as the nation's leaders seek to stabilize the economy and restore public trust and confidence.

On our own personal odyssey, we wanted to go beyond the common images of Greece to understand the deeper character and spirit of the Greek people, to understand their attitudes toward life and, of course, to share in their ageless wisdom. We wanted to understand how the Greeks were coping with, surviving, and even in some cases, thriving during this period of stress and uncertainty, so that we could share these lessons with others who may be facing similar circumstances in their own countries and lives. We wanted to learn how the Greeks were finding meaning in their everyday lives and work despite the chaos around them. Although our lives may appear to be very different from the indigenous people who live in the traditional Greek villages of today, at the basic human level they are the same. We are all trying to live the meaningful life.

Greece is a very special and sacred place. When we think of Greece, we often think of the whitewashed houses with blue doors and shutters painted to match the colors of the Greek national flag (and some say, reflecting the colors of the sea or sky). We think of the many islands where tiny fishing boats lay docked in the forefront of sandy beaches and vast rolling hills filled with olive groves. We think of the laughter of people as they gather to dine and dance with large groups of family and friends. And of course, we think of the origin of the Olympic Games.

Greece has also been honored as the birthplace or cradle of Western civilization. The Greeks were leaders who built the foundations in many areas, such as architecture, mathematics, medicine, music, politics (including democracy), science, theater, and many others, which established the *way* and *quality* of life that we experience and enjoy to this very day. Many of us are familiar with the stories of the Greek gods, such as Apollo, Atlas, Dionysus, Hades, Hercules, Hermes, Poseidon, and Zeus, and Greek goddesses like Aphrodite, Artemis, Athena, Demeter, Gaia, Hera, Hestia, and Hygeia. The ancient Greek philosophers, Pythagoras, Thales, Heraclitus, Socrates, Plato, Aristotle, Hypatia, and others, are well-known for their advanced views of the world and contributions to modern thinking. (The early "pre-Socratic" Greek philosophers, like Heraclitus, were contemporaries of the Indian spiritual teacher Siddhartha Gautama, the historical Buddha, and the Chinese philosophers Lao-tzu and Confucius; all offered complementary, if not alternative, perspectives on the meaning of life.) Greek was the common language of the Mediterranean countries and at least a third of all words we use in English are of Greek origin. In the now famous words of the English poet Percy Bysshe Shelley, written in 1821, "We are all Greeks. Our laws, our literature, our religion, our arts have their root in Greece."

Other countries and cultures have benefited from the foundation that the Greeks laid and have now raced ahead to achieve great success in the worlds of commerce, technology, and even politics. With its small population, Greece is overshadowed by the giants in today's commercial world—the United States, China, Japan, Brazil, Russia, etc. Although some say Greece peaked too early in the first Golden Age, approximately twenty-five hundred years ago, we believe that the second Golden Age of Greece is coming!

Understanding the Deeper Character

On our journey, we visited many traditional Greek villages and were treated with amazing hospitality. We were welcomed in to enjoy simple meals of feta cheese, olives, freshly baked bread, and ripe fruit and vegetables. We drank ouzo, raki, and red wine, and laughed and danced until the sun came up once again. We danced on the very beach where the character Zorba danced and felt the burdens of life lift from our shoulders. We rose at dawn to watch the fishermen return with their early morning catches. We walked in the footsteps of the Minoans and marveled at their high quality of life, lived so many millennia ago. We celebrated birthdays, "name days," weddings, and special holidays with feasts attended by extended families and people from neighboring villages. We sat with villagers of all ages to listen to their life stories. We explored, we listened, and we learned.

We discovered that it is an interesting time for everyone in Greece, given the recent challenges of the economic crisis and the austerity, or cost-cutting measures, implemented throughout the country. When we asked about these challenges, the villagers' responses revealed their unique and resilient spirit:

"Now we suffer but something good will come from this. We will make it through this, just as we have made it through other tough times in our history."

"We have each other. We can share our food with each other."

"Just as the olive tree can be cut in half through
its trunk and a new tree will grow from the cut, we
will grow once again after this cut."

Throughout our travels, we found that the people in the
traditional Greek villages spoke and lived simply but were
incredibly wise about life. They knew how to live with joy
and meaning. They knew how to build community, treat
one another well, and connect in authentic ways. They
knew how to embrace *all of life*—all the ups and downs,
all the difficulties and joys. They knew how to live not just
with their heads, but with their hearts and spirits as well.
And we also discovered that, even today, they know about
and practice the wisdom of the ancient Greek philosophers.

Join us on our odyssey as we share how the lessons
from the villagers and the ageless wisdom from the ancient
Greek philosophers provide the step-by-step formula for
how to live a meaningful life! Along the way, we've also
provided OPA! Affirmations, which can help guide you
to take more positive action in your life. In chapter two,
we explore the origins, history, and deeper meaning of the
common Greek word "OPA!" Then we share how the word
OPA! translates into a new lifestyle *and* work style, which
we call The OPA! Way.

OPA! AFFIRMATION

*I find joy and meaning in my life when I
view my life as a personal odyssey.*

2

OPA! More than a Word

It was a beautiful summer's evening and we were enjoying the fresh sea breeze blowing across the patio of the small restaurant nestled in the harbor. We were just finishing the last course of a wonderful feast of local food when our host stopped by our table.

"Tonight we have a special treat for you. Tonight we dance!" he said, glowing with pride, eager to share a bit of the traditional culture with us. In haste, several of the local men cleared away the empty tables and prepared a space for the dance. Slowly the Greek music filled the air and, one by one, the locals rose and joined in with the dance.

As is common with Greek dance, it starts small and ends big. With some urging from the more experienced Greek dancers, it doesn't take much time before "the dance" becomes a community affair. We joined in, awkwardly trying to follow the steps, but we focused more on the overall joy of the dance than on whether or not we missed a few steps or two.

Soon the Greek word "OPA!" filled the air, and everyone in the restaurant, including some international travelers who did not speak Greek, rose from their chairs and joined the line of dancers who, by now, were twisting and turning their way across the patio and through the restaurant tables. Everyone got involved since they all knew, without really knowing why or how, that "OPA!" is a call to action and a sign of belonging. It doesn't matter from what country you are or what native language you speak, when you hear "OPA!" you know what it means and you know what you must do: It's time to join in and dance with the rest of your Greek family!

OPA! and Greek Dancing

It is customary for Greeks to shout "OPA!" when dancing. You may have seen this happen at a Greek festival where dancers, dressed in traditional costumes from various parts of Greece, proudly and enthusiastically exhibit their dancing moves and athletic skills. You may have also seen such a display of the OPA! spirit when watching Greek dancing on television or in popular movies, such as *My Big Fat Greek Wedding* and *Mamma Mia!*

To Greeks, dance is not simply a recreational activity or a way to celebrate good times. On the contrary, the long-standing tradition of dance across Greece is a well-known part of their entire way of life; an authentic integration of mind, body, and spirit. Throughout the ages, Greek dance has proven to be not only a release or way to manage stress, but also an inspirational force that guides the Greeks *through* the stress so that they can confront—and ideally overcome—whatever challenges they are facing in life and work. Be it to deal with foreign occupations or economic crises, dance is built into the Greek culture's DNA and used not only as a weapon to combat adversity but also as a tool to build resilience.

In the famous novel *Zorba the Greek*, written by Nikos Kazantzakis, it was the dance that enabled Zorba to see through the fog of everyday life and inspired him and others to achieve their highest potential. The movie's classic song, "Zorba's Dance," is recognized worldwide as a powerful catalyst for making anyone, even the most reluctant or unwilling individual, want to dance. Indeed, just thinking about this song makes us feel like dancing like Zorba, and to do what has now become the custom: enthusiastically shout "OPA!"

You may have also heard the expression "OPA!" when someone drops a plate in a restaurant—either on purpose, as a symbol of celebration, or by accident. Or you may have heard everybody in a restaurant shout "OPA!" when the Greek cheese appetizer, Saganaki, is lit. ("Flaming" Saganaki is a predominantly North American invention of frying or grilling cheese, setting it aflame with brandy, and finally extinguishing the flames with lemon juice.)

The Origins and Meaning of OPA!

Interestingly, we've been able to trace the roots of the word "OPA!" to ancient Greece. Thanks to our dear friend Sophia Tsakiroglou Bothou, founder of the Athena Apollo Museum in Athens, we learned that the word can be found in both *The Iliad* and *The Odyssey*, which were written some three thousand years ago!

According to Greek mythology, nine goddesses or muses inspired the creation of literature and the arts. (Today, we often compliment a woman by referring to her as a "muse"; someone who inspires creativity.) The muse Kalliope had a beautiful voice and was best known as Homer's muse and his inspiration for *The Iliad* and *The Odyssey*. In Homer's epic writings, OPA! had the distinct meaning of "singing with a beautiful-sounding voice," with direct reference to the voice of Kalliope. The chanting or calling out to Kalli*ope* was shortened to "OPE!" and eventually that morphed into "OPA!" In time, the word began to describe the high tone of a vocalist who, through his or her "OPA!" was able to create an uplifting and enthusiastic spirit.

Today, there are many definitions and associated uses of OPA! Although it does not have an exact translation in English, it is a common Greek word used mosfrequently to express joy, excitement, and inspiration.When used as an expression, it reinforces the belief that ultimately, no matter how challenging our situation, we always have the freedom to choose our attitude—and exclaiming "OPA!" helps us choose a positive, resilient attitude. The word is also life-affirming, suggesting that, in one way or another, life truly matters and that all of life holds unlimited potential. Shouting "OPA!" lifts the spirits of the person saying it and it can also elevate the spirits of those who hear it. To be sure, it would be very difficult to shout out "OPA!" or to hear "OPA!" and not feel good about life!

We discovered while on our odyssey in Greece that the word "OPA!" also means different things to different people and its exact definition is often debated. Some Greeks told us that "OPA!" can be interpreted or translated into English to mean "what the hell, let's do it," which they viewed as an expression of freedom and self-reliance.

Another interpretation of the word was given to us by our good friend Andreas, the owner of the Greek restaurant Acropolis in Rethymno, Crete. With his usual passion and confidence, Andreas told us that "OPA!" can also mean "wake up," "danger," and "look out." In this interpretation, OPA! reminds us to remain awake and conscious of our life's journey so that we don't regret our choices later on, nor become like a fly stuck on the windowsill of life—wanting more out of life but unable to see or take advantage of the other options available to us.

Initially, we found Andreas' perspective on its use unusual, but as we later learned, it was based on an accurate definition, depending upon the word's actual spelling in the Greek language. There are two letters in the Greek alphabet that represent the single English letter "O": "O" (omicron) and "Ω" (omega). Spelled with an omicron, OPA! (ΌΠΑ) means *voice*, as we described with our story of Kalliope, along with excitement and spirit. However, when spelled with an omega, OPA! (ΩΠΑ), which is derived from various ancient Greek words describing the opening of our eyes, means "danger" or "watch out." So Andreas was very insightful when he told us that "OPA!" can express excitement but also "wake up!" or "look out!"

Our examination of OPA! from ancient times to the present day reveals that it can be viewed as two sides of the same coin:

- One side, ΌΠΑ, refers to the uplifting, *enthusiastic* expression that is often heard during some kind of celebration; a manifestation of "kefi" or spirit. (The word "enthusiasm" is from the Greek words "en" [in] and "theos" [god], essentially meaning "manifesting the spirit within.")
- The other, ΩΠΑ, refers to the human need to remain awake or *aware* and be on the lookout for any possible dangers, as well as opportunities, in one's life path.

Much like the Chinese concept of yin and yang, these two sides of the OPA! Coin may appear to be opposite life forces, but are actually interconnected and interdependent. Both sides are needed to build resilience, manage life transitions, and enjoy life to the fullest.

Two sides of the OPA! Coin

Our OPA! Moment

Of course, OPA! has a unique meaning for us. One day after traveling through the back roads of Crete, we stopped for a late dinner at a local taverna. We were just beginning to enjoy our mezedes (appetizers) when we were interrupted by shouts of "OPA!" coming from the other side of the taverna. We smiled at each other, raised our glasses of red wine in a toast, and echoed "OPA!" at our table. Call it synchronicity or whatever you wish but, as we began to discuss the results of our many interviews, we realized that the letters in OPA! just happened to relate to the three traits we found most prevalent in the people who felt they had the greatest meaning in their lives:

- They connect meaningfully with others.
- They engage with deeper purpose.
- They embrace life with attitude.

The initial letters in the words "others" (O), "purpose" (P), and "attitude" (A) spell the word and, coincidentally, form the acronym OPA! We felt our hearts start to beat faster and our faces light up with excitement. "OPA!" That was it! The Greeks we had talked to were truly manifesting an OPA! lifestyle. They were truly living The OPA! Way.

OPA! as a Path to Personal Growth

Sometimes, even though the world is so complex, the solutions to our challenges can actually be quite simple. As we turn to the Greeks to help us solve these challenges, we come full circle. Thousands of years ago, the Greeks led the way in discovering new ways to think and be in the world around them; today, we can turn to them once again to share their timeless wisdom about how we can live more joyful and meaningful lives.

What we find fascinating is that the ancient Greeks were leaders in holistic thinking—viewing the world from an integrated point of view, not just looking at the parts or events of our lives as being separate. They believed that nothing and no one was separate, that everything in the universe was connected. They were ahead of their time with their insights into the integration of body, mind, and spirit. (It was much later that the body and mind were viewed as separate entities, leading to what we believe are many of the issues we face in the pursuit of well-being today.)

The ancient Greeks were ahead of their time with their discoveries in the first Golden Age of Greece, some twenty-five hundred years ago. But many of us (including some Greeks of today) didn't listen to them. We went off on our path of individualism, the never-ending pursuit of material gain and wealth, and the pursuit of technology as the primary means of connecting. We separated mind, body, and spirit. Now stressed and overwhelmed, we are trying to find our way back and the traditional Greeks are waiting for us; they are waiting to help us deal with the economic crisis, they are waiting to help us build our resilience to deal with the destruction that we are witnessing in our world today, and they are waiting to help us return to the core essence of life. In many ways, the Greeks in the villages whom we met along our journey are now ahead of their time once again.

The Pursuit of Meaning

The challenge many of us face is that we are chasing goals, such as happiness, pleasure, and power, that aren't leading to deeper meaning in our lives. Importantly, The OPA! Way is not about the pursuit of happiness per se. Many have quoted Aristotle as saying that the goal of all human activity is to achieve happiness. As we share in chapter eight, Aristotle's thoughts on this subject are often misquoted and misunderstood. Happiness is not the ultimate goal of life. Happiness is an emotion that is linked to pleasure but it is fleeting; it doesn't last. We can share a happy moment when we are enjoying a good meal or a good laugh with a friend, but this emotion lasts only a short time. It is an illusion to believe that "the pursuit of happiness" will bring us a deep sense of meaning in life.

The OPA! Way is not about the pursuit of power or influence either. Power is about being strong and dominant, having (or trying to have) control over others or other things. Ultimately, though, the pursuit of power leads to emptiness because power over others or over our circumstances in life is just another illusion. Our only real power lies *within* ourselves. It can also be said that the pursuit of power is less likely than the pursuit of pleasure (or happiness) to lead to meaning and, for all practical purposes, is even farther removed from it.

The OPA! Way is also not about the pursuit of wealth, which in itself is a primitive form of the pursuit of power.

We've all heard people express the idea that more wealth will bring them both happiness and meaning: "If only I had more money." But the results of many research studies have shown that once we achieve a certain level of wealth, enough to cover the basics of life, any increase in new wealth does not necessarily result in a lot more satisfaction. In other words, doubling our money won't bring about a doubling of meaning in our lives.

The OPA! Way is about the pursuit of *meaning* in our lives. Having deep meaning in our lives helps us enjoy life despite the ups and downs, the joys and the difficulties, we may experience. Meaning gives us a sense of fulfillment and a passion for life. Meaning helps us build resilience.

Meaning helps us live all of life to the fullest with enthusiasm. Meaning is the fuel that keeps the human spirit moving forward at *all* times, not just during the good times.

Our mission is to help you live a more meaningful life by applying the ageless wisdom of The OPA! Way paradigm and lifestyle. Throughout this book, we share our journey, our adventures, our challenges, and our learning with you. The three core lessons we discovered throughout our odyssey, along with the ways to practice them, can be found in parts two through four, under Others, Purpose, and Attitude, respectively. So, read on and discover how you can live and work with joy and meaning. OPA!

OPA! AFFIRMATION

I find joy and meaning in my life when I live and work The OPA! Way.

Part Two

OTHERS (O):
Connect Meaningfully
with Others

3

Connect with *The Village*

Yesterday we visited the small traditional village of Vrisses, located in the mountainous central region of the island of Crete. We knew from past visits that there was only one very narrow road that wound through the village like a snake, so we chose to be respectful and park our car at the bottom of the village and walk. (We have rarely encountered another car, but if we had, we would have found it extremely difficult to reverse ours without leaving a dint in the wall of someone's house!)

We climbed the first set of stairs and stopped to catch our breath when we reached the first landing. We continued our journey, climbing another set of stairs fashioned from a mixture of stones and concrete, using the handrail to pull ourselves up the very steep incline. When we stopped to rest again, a tiny old woman passed us, dressed in black from head to toe and laden with two bags overflowing with the greens she must have just picked from the hillside. She smiled and said, "Yiasas." (This is a common greeting used in Greece and literally means, "To your health.") We echoed her greeting, smiled, and realized that she was probably thirty years older and definitely in much better shape than we were from climbing these stairs on a daily basis in the fresh mountain air.

We continued our ascent and gave thanks to the person who installed the railing fashioned from old pipes, a necessity on rainy or snowy days, and, of course, for visitors like us. We turned the corner and finally reached our destination—the home of YiaYia (Grandmother) Maria. There she was, standing in the doorway of her small home, her eyes twinkling with life, all five feet of her. Of course, she was also dressed in black, the national color and uniform of older Greek women. Her silver-gray hair was tied back neatly in a bun, secured with numerous bobby pins.

"Welcome, welcome," she said with a wide smile and outstretched arms, as she ushered us into her home, a one-room house of roughly four hundred square feet. The house was sparsely decorated with a single bed, a small wooden table, three old woven thatched chairs where generations before had sat, a cooking area with a single sink, a small cabinet that held dishes, provisions and teas stored for the winter, and, hanging on the whitewashed walls, a few photos of her family. In another corner were the recent additions of a television and telephone.

Everything in Maria's home has its purpose. We always struggle with what to bring as a present for Maria—what do we buy a woman who looks like she has nothing in comparison to the goods available in our shopping malls in America, but who, in actuality, has everything she needs? We handed her the fresh fruit we had purchased in the city. We knew full well that she had access to many different varieties of fruit and vegetables only steps from her home, so we also brought her a few treats from the bakery.

YiaYia Maria had been busy all day preparing a simple feast for us and the other five relatives who had also come to visit. Her table was overflowing with fresh food to share— thinly sliced cucumbers, cubes of feta cheese, plump red tomatoes, beans, beets, potatoes drenched in olive oil and oregano, olives, slices of freshly baked bread, apples, oranges, nuts, and, of course, small cheese pies for dessert—all served with an abundance of love. Yes, we felt like we were home.

Since there were only three chairs in the room, the other "girls" (Yia Yia Maria, her two daughters, and two granddaughters) sat on the edge of the bed. The conversation flowed easily with Yia Yia Maria's positive energy filling the room. As we were enjoying our feast, Yia Yia Maria noticed a hole in the knee of her granddaughter's jeans. "I will sew that for you," she offered, but was quickly refuted.

"That's fashion, Yia Yia!" responded the granddaughter, eliciting a round of laughter.

"Do you want more food, Yia Yia?" asked her granddaughter.

"No thanks," she replied; "I'm watching my figure." She burst out laughing again, rolling backward on the bed. She was almost eighty but had the spirit and energy of youth.

A few hours later, the gathering came to an end and we all said our good-byes. Of course, Yia Yia Maria handed us a few extra cheese pies to take with us on our journey. As we descended the hill, holding onto the railing once again, we remarked to each other about what a wonderful visit it had been. We've been to gatherings in homes many times larger than Yia Yia Maria's was, equipped with many more so-called amenities, but we have never experienced the feelings of warmth and belonging as we did on that day. Once again, our visit to the village of Vrisses had reminded us of the value of living in and connecting meaningfully with others in the village.

Humanity

We can use the concept of "village" to define many groups of people—from a few family members to a collection of people living in a neighborhood, organization, city, or even nation. What makes a village is *not* the number of people or the buildings or the possessions of its members, but the energy that is shared between the people who choose to belong to that village. It's their energy, which is breathed into the space. Importantly, their energy can be positive or negative—both good and bad can spread throughout any village.

"All is One."
—PARMENIDES

In a deeper metaphysical sense, a collective life is created in the village. Life is reflective. Life in the village reflects the belief, "I *am* **because** of *you*. I am more of myself because I am connected to others in our village, be it the village where I live or where I work." For YiaYia Maria, she *is* because she is a part of the village. Living her life in the village of Vrisses gives Maria a deep sense of humanity, belonging, and meaning. And like YiaYia Maria, many Greeks we met along our way shared their need to be authentically and meaningfully connected; to be a part of the whole.

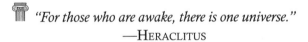

"For those who are awake, there is one universe."
—HERACLITUS

People come to Greece for many reasons—some to enjoy the serenity of the blue sky and pristine water, some to walk in the footsteps of the ancients and, of course, some to drink ouzo and indulge in the delicious food. We come to Greece because of the people. For us, the people we meet are very real.

In America, we are used to people asking us, "What do you do?" The answer to this question tends to categorize people into social classes and achievement levels. However, in Greece, we found that conversations go to the very soul of the people. In Greece, we were asked questions that focused on *who* we were. "What village are you from?" is a typical question that serves both to understand one's roots but also is a means to find a common connection:

"My family originates from the village of Monastiraki in the Amari Valley."

"Ah, Amari—you are near me—I am from the same valley."

The conversation helps people connect on a human level. Making you feel comfortable, asking about roots, and establishing the human connection comes first; asking about work and accomplishments comes later.

During a conversation with a young woman named Violetta, who was seated beside us on an Aegean Airlines flight back to Athens, we shared that we had just traveled around Crete and loved a little village named Plaka. "Plaka, my mother is from Plaka! Did you know there are only fifteen full-time residents when the tourists leave in the winter?" she replied, her eyes showing absolute delight. During another chance meeting, this time with Iakovos Pattakos, a relative, his introduction was telling: "You are Pattakos. I am Pattakos. We are Pattakos." With these words, he quickly established the bond that will last a lifetime!

Everyone tries to find a connection somewhere in the lineage where you might be a cousin, a distant relative, or know someone they know. Hearing the word "cousin" shouted in a crowded room results in many people turning their heads to see if you are, indeed, the cousin they are looking for. Everyone may be your cousin! If you are not Greek, the same philosophy applies: "Where are you from? Ah, you are from Chicago. I have cousins Nick, Nicki, and Niko in Chicago. Perhaps you know them?" In some way, they will always find a connection, a common bond.

The Human Touch

Throughout Greece we noticed that building relationships through conversation was an integral part of daily activity. Our business meeting in Athens began with the grandfather and son of the owner spending time with us discussing our odyssey while sharing water, coffee, and cookies—an example of "the human touch before the task." The clerk in the local grocery store in the picturesque town of Hania, Crete, engaged in a long conversation with the young woman in front of us in line, while we and everyone else waited patiently. Although we may have wanted to pay for our purchases quickly, we all knew that the store was an important connection point in the community and that the clerk was taking an interest in her customers as people and not just as business transactions—again, "the human touch before the task."

It's about the conversation and the connection. Stopping to say hello to others acknowledges their presence—their human existence—and signals to them that they are an important part of the village. Every interaction is an opportunity to strengthen or weaken connections with others. Little by little, with each interaction, meaningful relationships are built.

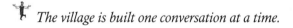 *The village is built one conversation at a time.*

During one of our visits with YiaYia Maria, she shared her dislike for large cities where she felt it was difficult to connect with others. She told us she would walk down the street and look someone straight in the eye but they would just look away. She found it interesting that on one hand we all say we yearn to connect on a human level, but then we avoid the connection that is right in front of us, that is right beside us on the bus or train, that is right in our neighborhood. We choose instead to give a quick wave and disappear into our house or to simply look away.

The Plaka *and the* Volta

Many villages in Greece are designed around a common *plaka*, or public square, where people routinely gather to meet and socialize instead of sitting alone in their homes. It is both a physical place as well as a symbolic place since it serves to remind everyone in the village that they are all one, that they are connected, and that they are part of something larger than themselves.

The Greek word for the evening stroll is "volta," which has a dual purpose of reenergizing (hence, the English word "voltage") and connecting with others. As our friend Nikos told us, "Greeks are happy because we go out after work and connect instead of going home and watching television." Many an evening we witnessed old men walking together, children running free while a dozen women sitting on nearby benches watched, and young men pushing their toddlers in strollers, deep in conversation.

Always *Time for* Coffee

Another timeless tradition is visiting the *kafenio* (café), the heart of the village. Rarely do people carry coffee around in a cup—they sit and relax and enjoy the coffee instead. Greek men typically meet at the kafenio up to three times a day: in the early morning, late afternoon, and the evening. In small villages there may be only one kafenio, but in larger villages numerous *kafenia* spring up, even if they are only the front room of a house, with additional tables and chairs spilling onto the roadway. The tables are littered with small coffee cups, filled to the rim with brown foam. In between small sips, the villagers celebrate the highlights as well as release the stresses of the day.

Regulars, usually older men, make one kafenio in the village their "home away from home," and they go to this same location every day to read newspapers, argue politics, play cards, and discuss their lives. Some Greeks, even in the large cities, such as Athens, may have five or six coffees throughout the day as they take time to connect with various people at different kafenia.

There's always time for coffee but, as we all know, it's not about the coffee, it's about the conversation and bonding that takes place while enjoying the coffee. Some say the male bonding at the kafenio—as it is mostly men who partake in this Greek tradition—is a key factor in the longevity of its patrons as they take care of one another and have trust that there will always be someone there for them. Nothing creates the meaningful connection and knowledge of shared humanity like speaking with other people and seeing the expressions on their faces. Nothing is better than knowing that we are all still human after all!

Belonging

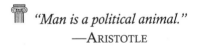 *"Man is a political animal."*
—ARISTOTLE

The word "political" comes from the Greek word "polis," meaning "city" or "state." Putting it in modern terms, when Aristotle said, "Man is a political animal," he meant we are social animals or beings and we flourish best in groups or communities (villages). It is our nature to live in groups and it is our nature to want to belong. We are not at our best when we isolate ourselves. One of the causes of the increased incidence of depression throughout the world is the lack of belonging. Some say that as we age, the longing for connections with others deepens, but we disagree. Our research has shown us that the quest to connect and belong, the longing for the security and comfort provided by groups, is strong at *all* ages.

"I am not alone in my fear, nor alone in my hope, nor alone in my shouting."
—NIKOS KAZANTZAKIS (author, *Zorba the Greek*)

We live in the global community but many people feel separate and alone. Connecting online may mean having eight hundred "friends" on Facebook, or being able to "tweet" thousands of "followers" via Twitter, yet we question whether these connections enable us to share who we authentically are or, importantly, the challenges we face in our lives. Are we just technically connected but not meaningfully connected?

The ancient Greek philosopher Thales suggested that we should "love thy neighbor," but how can we love our neighbors when we don't even know them? We know the names of celebrities but we don't know the names of our neighbors. It takes effort to know our neighbors and for them to know us.

"We are all One," espoused Heraclitus, but nowadays we often look and act separately from one another. We say we don't feel part of a community because we aren't. We are more mobile these days, leading nomadic lives, moving often, working long hours, commuting, and staying indoors watching television or distracted by the internet, downloading movies instead of going out. And in times of crisis, we tend to draw inward to try and isolate ourselves from outside forces, attempting to create a sense of security. But we found that even during times of financial and social crisis in Greece, there is still a strong need to reach out and connect meaningfully with others, to strengthen the sense of belonging.

Do You Know Aunt Toula?

In many Greek villages and even towns, there are no numbers on the houses because everyone knows where everyone else lives. When arriving in the village, you simply describe who you are looking for and a kind villager will either provide directions to where you must go or stop whatever he or she is doing and take you there in person. While in Crete, we wanted to visit one of our many aunts, Aunt Toula, but we weren't sure which house in the village was hers. So we showed a photo of her to some local villagers and they brought us to her house. We wondered if someone had shown us a photo of one of our neighbors or coworkers, would we have known where to find that person?

"We should look for someone to eat and drink with before looking for something to eat and drink."
—EPICURUS

Food!

Some say everything happens around food in Greece! It may be more accurate to say everything happens around food, coffee, wine, and ouzo (or raki, the regional drink of Crete) but, in any case, it is while eating and drinking that Greeks connect. Again, it's not all about the food—it's about the people you eat with and the conversation and bonding that being together brings with it. Who you eat with is just as important as what you eat!

Food is the central focus of the family home, with most Greek mothers providing both food and nurturing to a home full of family and friends. No matter what time of day you arrive, there will always be food available. "Eat something. I'll make you something special" are words we hear often. After

34

years of being occupied by foreign powers and being deprived of basic necessities, the Greeks know very well that food is the basis of living and that people will always connect over food. Again, during the current crisis, we see the focus returning to food as the primary basic need, as well as the way for people to connect meaningfully with one another. Financial resources may be strained, luxury goods may remain on the store shelves, but food is the one thing that unites the village.

"*Fifteen pounds of flour?*" we asked, thinking it was a lot (almost 7 kg of flour) and that Alex's mother had made a mistake in her recipe. "Yes, fifteen pounds," she confirmed and continued listing the rest of the ingredients we would need to make the traditional *koulourakia* or Easter cookies. Oh yes, it was we who had forgotten—when baking, always make enough for the village; always make enough to share. Baking for the holidays is usually a group effort when the ladies in the village get together to socialize and make hundreds of cookies for the upcoming feast. Each person usually has her own family recipe, which was handed down to her through the ages, so it's always an interesting affair to hear the debate: "Add more sugar." "No, don't add any more sugar." "We use more cinnamon." In the democracy that *is* Greece, indeed, everyone has their say.

One might say the Easter feast is the largest celebration of the year, but that is only if one hasn't been to a local wedding that year, especially on the island of Crete where wedding parties in the city can grow to over a thousand well-wishers. It's not uncommon to have large wedding parties with more than sixteen people in the bridal party because, after all, everyone is a cousin! It's not unusual to go to the taverna and invite everyone in the whole village to the wedding and to put an open announcement in the local newspaper. It is the community that celebrates the wedding. There will be enough bread and cheese for everyone.

There will be lamb on the spit and enough food to feed the army of wedding guests. Yes, food from many homes will be emptied onto platters and passed down the long tables set up in the village square or *plateia*. When, thousands of years ago, Cleobulus advised that moderation is best, he certainly wasn't referring to the food at a Greek wedding!

"Food brings us together around the table," explained Stavros as we shared the community table with him in a local taverna in the hillsides of Crete. "We never eat alone and we never eat in silence; well, except for the monks at Mount Athos," he continued with a twinkle in his eye. As we looked around the rustic taverna we saw tables occupied by people of all ages—young children with their great grandparents and workmen in their overalls, covered with evidence of a hard day's work, sharing the table with people whose attire signaled a more leisurely life.

On the community tables were a variety of large platters of appetizers (mezes or mezedes) and salads next to baskets brimming with freshly baked whole-grain breads and bottles of local olive oil. Everyone appeared to be savoring the food—sharing from common platters, not individual plates and portions. Everyone appeared to be savoring the conversations. The food and laughter were plentiful, symbolizing the simple pleasure of sharing a meal with friends in the presence of community.

The tradition of kerasmata, the buying of drinks for others, also united the taverna. The two men sitting off to the side, tossing their komboloi (worry beads) and watching a game on the television, stopped to share in a drink of ouzo or raki offered by some men at another table.

"Yamas (to our health)," said the pair as they raised their glasses. Giving a nod to the other men, they drank and resumed watching their game. Twenty minutes later, it was

their turn to order a round of drinks for themselves and the other table, and the yamas exercise continued.

Interdependence

During our most recent travels throughout Greece, we observed a positive and meaningful albeit unintended result of Greece's economic crisis: the *rediscovery* of the importance of the village! We've talked at length with both young people and older adults who not only are spending more time in their family's village (*horio*), but also are investing considerable energies and resources to renovate structures and community infrastructure in the village. Besides seeking a reprieve from the chaos associated with living in highly populated areas, which are most negatively influenced by the current economic situation, these returning villagers are focusing more on the things that truly matter to them by essentially returning to their "roots."

We asked many Greeks: "Why do you seem so resilient during this economic crisis?" More often than not, their responses centered on the beliefs that they could always go back to their villages, and that their grandparents (especially their grandmothers!) and extended families would care for them, and that they, in turn, would do the same. They knew that, at the very least, there would be food in the villages for all so that they all could survive.

Most of the food is grown or raised locally. Eggs, milk, cheese, fruit, vegetables, wine, olives, olive oil, and meat (sheep or rabbit) are all items traded amongst the families in the village. As our cousin Elsa told us, "We never bought eggs, there was always someone who had eggs to share." For other items, they rely on traders who travel between villages in the area with large cars filled with bread, fish, and household items.

37

Relying on others is a shared value of the village. A woman we visited in Elounda, Crete, told us that she was going to Athens for a month. "But what about your child?" we asked. Her reply was telling, "There are many people in my village to look after my child while I am away," she said with confidence. Her reply reminded us of the time we were in church when a small boy, probably age three or four, insisted on blowing out some of the small candles people were holding during the service. No less than three older women, all dressed in black, told him to behave. They didn't hold back; they were active participants in shaping the character of this child and in creating the type of village they wanted. They supported the notion that it takes a village to raise a child.

The spirit of cooperation was alive and well when we visited the small, more modern village of Kalives. We were enjoying a late afternoon coffee at the kafenio on the narrow street that flows through the village, leisurely watching both time and people go by. The noise of the regional bus coming down the street broke the silence. Suddenly, the bus stopped and we realized that it was unable to pass by because a motorcycle was jutting out into the road. Three local men jumped into action. One helped the bus driver back the large bus up a few feet while the other two moved the motorcycle off the road. Then, inch-by-inch the bus moved forward and around the motorcycle and eventually was able to be on its way. The event provided ten minutes of excitement before we all went back to enjoying our afternoon coffees, reflecting on the knowledge that life requires a group effort.

"He who cares for his brother cares for himself."
—XENOPHON

Today, instead of being connected to the others we know for the necessities of life, we rely on strangers and institutions for our survival. We seldom barter with a neighbor or even know where our food is grown or comes from; we usually rely on a weekly transaction at a supermarket for everything, including our eggs! We seldom rely on others for our news, we rely on the internet. Elders seldom stay in the family home; they are checked into "old age" homes. We also now rely more on ourselves, resulting in a false sense of security. Instead of borrowing tools from our neighbors, we simply buy our own. Instead of asking others to help us, we simply do the chore ourselves. In doing so, what have we lost? Have we tried so hard to be self-sufficient that we cut ourselves off from one another? Perhaps if we had less financial wealth and material possessions, we would have to rely on others more, like the Greeks in the village do.

An old man gave each son a stick. "Break them," he said to his sons. Each son easily broke his own stick. Next the old man took several sticks and tied them together in a bundle. He handed the bundle to his first son and commanded, "Break it." Unable to do so, the first son passes the bundle to the second son. One by one each son strained to break the bundle but was unable to do so. **Union gives strength.** Divided we are weak and vulnerable; but together we are strong. There is strength in numbers if we "stick" together.
—*Aesop's Fables* (Greece, ca 620–560 BC)

Survival in the traditional Greek village depends on collective strength of the villagers, not the strength of one individual. This structure gives each villager a sense of comfort; villagers know that their family and village will be there to care for them. This mentality arose out of their historical struggles—throughout many wars, foreign occupations, and changes in government regimes, they had to rely on one another for survival.

Asking for help does not show weakness; it shows a deeper understanding of the concept of interdependence and the inherent strength that comes with it.

The village is the sum of all who live there. It is the sum of all their thoughts and actions. As a member of the village, it is one's duty to take an active role in supporting it. In good times and in troubled times, villagers rely on their shared purpose and allegiance to the village. An ancient phrase known to many Greeks is "help me so I can help you so that together we can climb the mountain." Your success is our success *and* our success is your success. The spirit of the village manifests itself as a "win-win," because villagers realize that it is in their individual and collective best interests to connect meaningfully with one another. In this way, the whole truly is greater than the sum of its parts.

We know every person influences the village, either positively or negatively, as his or her good or bad behavior ripples through the village. Everyone makes a difference and everyone has an impact. Even if someone tries to stay neutral or even disengaged, this attitude also makes a difference to the whole. The village is like an ecosystem in nature, interconnected, inseparable parts of the whole.

But which takes priority—the village or the individual? The ancient Greeks valued the individual and strongly believed that all individuals must make the effort to become the best they can be. They also valued private ownership of property and, of course, were well-known for introducing the concept of democracy (one person, one vote) to the world. To them, individual identity (and freedom) was very important and needed to be protected.

Over time, however, we have swung the pendulum so far toward the individual that some have classified our society as suffering from hyperindividualism. When we embrace too much focus on the individual, we disregard the impact that our thoughts, words, and actions have on the collective, which leads to the fragmentation of the whole and, eventually, to isolation, loneliness, and even depression. When we get lost in big cities, we no longer feel the loyalty to or *connection* with others, and engage in expressions of selfishness, such as graffiti, rioting, and crime. When we get lost in big companies or governments, we no longer feel connected and are less willing to make any sacrifices for the good of the group or our customers. We believe in "me first" and may even decide to make our own rules.

It's a delicate balance to define the self within the context of cooperation with others. We need both separation and togetherness to thrive. But if we don't emphasize what *connects* us, we will be divided. If we don't look out for the village, then the benefits of the village begin to erode and the ultimate meaning of self suffers as a consequence.

> *"He who is unable to live in society, or who has no need because he is sufficient for himself, must be either a beast or a god."*
> —ARISTOTLE

Summary

The urges to connect and to belong are the most basic of human needs and are central to the human experience. Aristotle taught us that we are political (social) animals—

we thrive when we connect. The ancient Greeks also believed that we are all connected to the energy of a larger system, to a greater whole. Importantly, the root of many of our challenges today can be traced to a lack of *meaningful* connections with others. The antidote for this lack of connection, loneliness, and isolation is to reach outside ourselves and invest our energies in creating better "villages," both at work and at home. In no small way, the depth of our lives depends on the depth of our relationships with others. Meaning is found in the context of our day-to-day lives, connecting with others. We will have meaning in our lives as long as others need us and we need them.

OPA! AFFIRMATION

I find joy and meaning in my life when I connect meaningfully with others in the village.

4

Connect with *Hospitality*

We have a weakness for fresh seafood, and during one trip to Greece, we had what we referred to as a spiritual experience, indulging in the best octopus we'd ever eaten. Our evening began with a leisurely stroll along the beachfront into the historic old town of Rethymno, where the narrow streets and alleyways take one back in time. We stumbled upon Cavo D'oro, a tiny restaurant nestled in the picturesque old harbor. Comfortably seated with a view of the pristine water, we noticed that a small blue and white boat moored in the water close to the restaurant was for sale.

"Should we buy it?" we joked with each other. When our waiter, Giorgos, stopped by our table to welcome us, we ordered several small dishes, including the now famous grilled octopus, and added, "And we'll take the boat!"

That began an evening of conversation with Giorgos; Petros, the owner of Cavo D'oro; and his father, Vasilis. The evening flew by as we all laughed and shared stories from our lives, savoring the impressive food, the soothing atmosphere, and most of all, the hospitality. As we walked back to our hotel in the cool night breeze, we remarked how wonderful our adventure to Cavo D'oro had been, especially in comparison to other dining experiences when we simply ordered, ate, and left.

Early the next morning, we chose to skip breakfast and set out on our journey to the beautiful Amari Valley, located in the central mountainous area of Crete. As our car weaved through the small village of Thronos, we decided to stop, stretch our legs, and take a look around. A few yards ahead we saw a sign, "Aravanes," that was painted on a piece of wood, with a large arrow pointing straight ahead. Curious, we followed the narrow pathway and arrived at the back of a building that appeared to be a small hotel, and gasped at the magnificent view of the Amari Valley that was laid out before us. We wandered inside and were greeted by Lambros, the owner.

"Yiasas, welcome," he said. He was busy setting up the restaurant for the day, but within a few minutes following our introductions and establishing that we were visiting Alex's homeland, he set three shot glasses on the bar and quickly filled them with homemade raki. (The offering of raki is a symbolic gesture welcoming one in from their journey as well as a gesture of celebration or friendship.)

"Yamas," we said in unison before downing the raki in one gulp and slamming the shot glasses back onto the bar.

Later, when we informed Lambros that we had to be on our way, he said, "Wait, I want to give you something—here is a book about the region." Returning to our car, we reflected on what a wonderful man Lambros was . . . and that we really should have eaten breakfast before setting out; a little bread and honey would have been good protection against the raki in our empty stomachs!

Continuing on our journey, we arrived at a crossroads where a small kafenio was located. As we weren't sure which road to take, we decided to stop and ask the men gathered together in front of the kafenio. We introduced ourselves and shared that we were looking for the road to the village of Monastiraki, the birthplace of Alex's pappou (grandfather).

"Please sit," gestured one man as the other yelled something into the kafenio. Soon the shot glasses and raki arrived at our table and the round of "yamas" echoed throughout the kafenio. We thought to ourselves, once again, "We really must have breakfast before we set out on our adventures!"

Following a short conversation, we again asked which road would take us to Monastiraki. Instead of simply pointing to the right road, one fellow jumped up and signaled for us to follow him—he would show us the way. We followed his truck up a winding dirt road and, after a few turns, the road opened up into the quaint village of Monastiraki. When we stopped our car, our guide motioned for us to follow him to his home. He insisted that we sit at his kitchen table, upon which he took out his carving knife and began to peel two apples for us. "Ah good, some breakfast," we thought to ourselves, knowing that the apples would help soak up the raki in our empty stomachs! Our host handed us the apples, which we gladly accepted. He also gave us two large oranges to take with us on our journey.

As we sat at our kind host's kitchen table, we reflected on the last twenty-four hours: beginning with our dining experience at Cavo D'oro, to meeting Lambros in Thronos, to meeting the men at the kafenio, and finally . . . to sitting in the home of a fellow we had just met by the roadside, who had shared raki with us and shown us the way to the village of Monastiraki, and who was intent on making sure that we had something to eat. We couldn't have been more grateful for these wonderful examples of authentic Greek hospitality!

Philoxenia

The word "philosophy" is derived from the Greek words "philos," meaning love, and "sophia" meaning wisdom, so philosophy is really the love of wisdom. In similar fashion, the word "philoxenia" is derived from philos (love) and the Greek word for stranger, "xenos." So philoxenia, as it relates to the concept of hospitality, is the love of strangers. Its roots can be traced back to the myths of the Greek god Zeus, referred to as "Zeus Xenios," who was the king of the gods and also the god of hospitality and protector of travelers. The English words "host," "hotel," and "hospital," it is interesting to note, are derived from the very same concept—that is, to take good care of strangers or guests.

There is a saying in Greece that if you are ever lost, you can just knock on someone's door and he or she will help you. The true meaning of Greek hospitality involves making sure the guest feels protected and taken care of and, at the end of the encounter, even providing guidance to the guest's next destination.

The Greeks we met along our journey told us that they believed all things, and thus all people, were connected and that they had a duty to ensure the health and well-being of others, especially during a crisis. "We are born to help one another," they told us. "In your family, it is expected, you have to do it; and for strangers, especially those who are tired and need help, it is your obligation to be hospitable."

 "It is the task of a good man to help those in misfortune."
—SOPHOCLES

Kindness

Once upon a time, a lion captured a small mouse in his large paw. Just as the lion was about to eat the mouse, the mouse exclaimed, "Stop, I may be able to do you a favor one day." The lion thought this was amusing as he doubted how a small mouse would be able to do him a favor, but he let the mouse go.

> *Sometime later, the lion was caught in a rope trap set by hunt-ers. The mouse, seeing the plight the lion was in, began to gnaw the ropes and eventually freed the lion. "See," said the mouse, "wasn't I right?!"* **No act of kindness, no matter how small, is ever wasted.**
>
> —*Aesop's Fables* (Greece, ca 620–560 BC)

We were the recipients of many acts of kindness during our odyssey. For example, when we were in Athens at the Megaro Mousiki metro stop, unsure of which line to take to our destination, a kind woman named Lida offered to help us. Coincidentally, as our destination just happened to be the same stop as hers was, she helped us purchase our tickets from the machine, ensured we followed her to the right train, and even walked us up to the street level and pointed us in the right direction. Despite living in the big city of Athens, where everything seems to move at least twice the pace of life on the islands, Lida still embodied the traditional values of Greek hospitality.

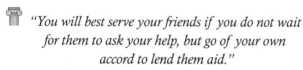

"You will best serve your friends if you do not wait for them to ask your help, but go of your own accord to lend them aid."
—Isocrates

Just as others have helped us in the past, we must help the next person. We need to keep the kindness circulating; to pay it forward. As global villagers, we are all born with the capacity to search for ways to help others and to spread kindness in the world. Living and working with meaning involves more than just satisfying our own needs. A truly meaningful life, including a meaningful work life, requires that we look out for the interests of others in addition to our own. In this connection, if we want more humane villages within which to live, we need to be more kind. Similarly, if we want more humane workplaces within which to work, we also need to be more kind.

What you do for others, you do for yourself.
TRADITIONAL VILLAGE WISDOM

Being kind requires empathy, the ability to identify and find resonance with someone else's situation or feelings. Being kind requires the awareness that we are all connected in some way. If we are willing and able to see ourselves reflected in the other person who needs help, then we can also see that we too may need help. The more aware we are of this interconnection and reflection of our shared humanity, the more kind we will be.

"If we always helped one another, no one would need luck."
—MENANDER

Generosity

One day we passed a large sign on the national highway just outside the town of Agia Pelagia, but were unable to read the sign because we were driving very fast. We circled back and had to smile when we saw the sign up close. While most signs tend to communicate one or two things, this sign was advertising not two, not five, not ten, but about twenty services offered in the nearby town, such as the availability of a hotel, supermarket, barber shop, taxi service, and jeweler's shop, along with goods like handbags, ties, vases, and fuel. We smiled because we knew that this was not just a physical sign on the highway but also a sign of Greek generosity. This sign symbolized the Greek's approach to life: We welcome you. We want to take care of you. We have plenty to share with you. We live in abundance!

Giving generously is a virtue that leads to deeper meaning in our lives, as we gain a sense of joy and fulfillment in giving to and taking care of others. It's the pride we take in opening our hearts and sharing what we have with others. It's the sense of satisfaction that we feel when we spend less time protecting ourselves and more time giving to others.

Hospitality reflects the generosity of the person and is a manifestation of the human spirit. However, we all know people who do not reflect true hospitality and, instead, expect others to cater only to their needs. We all know people who feel entitled to receive things. We hear them say, "I want" or "I deserve" or "You owe me" or "The government owes me." But as our friend Kostas advised us, it is better to always give more in value than you take.

Fortunately, there are a lot of generous people in the world who know that life is about feeling joy and sharing joy with others in the world. As we experienced in Greece, there's always room for one more, there's always food to share, there's always inviting conversation to join. Generosity, in other words, means that there's always a way to connect meaningfully with others!

One of the most special chance meetings we had in Greece was with a man named Kyriakos. After visiting the grave of a deceased relative in a small Cretan village, we were heading back to our car when a man approached us and, without even knowing who we were except that we were strangers in his village, invited us into his home for lunch. We protested, saying we had to be on our way but, as is the usual response, he ignored us and kept grabbing at our sleeves, pulling us into his home—gently, of course!

We relented and entered through the weather-beaten doors into the courtyard of his home. In the entrance was an old oven, which probably had served as the main cooking area for a century or two. Beside the oven was a table with several chairs where Kyriakos motioned for us to sit. Once seated, he and his wife served us raki and a wonderful feast of marinated meat, grilled potatoes, sliced cucumbers, fresh bread, and chocolate cookies.

Kyriakos took a keen interest in why we were at the gravesite and how we could be related in some way to the members of his village. When our collective attempts to determine our relationship with the deceased relative stumbled due to our collective broken English and Greek, he simply picked up his cell phone and called a friend in Athens who spoke many languages and could easily translate our conversation for us. After thirty minutes, we were all satisfied that we had figured out the family tree, and then it was time for us to continue on our journey. We couldn't leave his house without receiving a souvenir bottle of his homemade wine. And, of course, our visit wasn't complete until we also had a stop at his brother's house for a bottle of his homemade wine too. Again, we had experienced the true meaning of Greek hospitality firsthand.

Throughout our travels we were invited into many people's homes to share simple meals or were given food to ensure we did not go hungry. Penelope in Pyrgos, Santorini, made sure we continued on our way with a large bag of cookies. An older woman in the village of Chromonastiri, Crete, first offered us raki, then water, then a cookie, and then made sure we went on our way with an orange, which just happened to be the biggest orange we had ever seen. In another village, Stelios made sure we had a drink of freshly squeezed fruit juice before we continued on our journey and Costas, who runs one of the oldest bakeries in the old town of Rethymno, made sure we didn't leave without two of his extraordinary cookies, masterly fashioned into the shape of swans.

The concept of hospitality is deeply rooted in the rituals that are expressions of an authentic relationship between a host and guests or strangers based on generosity, curiosity, and friendship. This concept also extends to Greek restaurants, where going to a restaurant is like being welcomed into a Greek home; they want to ensure first that you feel comfortable and then you will eat! We observed that many of the Greek waiters spent time talking with their customers and also made sure everyone's glass was always full. The restaurant manager or owner visits each table, greeting everyone and connecting with them on a human level. (Although, of course, we have seen this happen in restaurants in our hometown in the United States, it often looks like it is done as a chore rather than with pleasure.) Unlike many other places where your dinner is rushed and you are handed the bill at the end of finishing your last bite, if not before, the attitude in Greece is very different. "Sit and enjoy your dinner, don't rush, let your food digest. Enjoy your time with us," said many waiters to us.

One of our favorite family-run tavernas is the Acropolis restaurant, located near the Aegean Pearl Hotel in Rethymno, Crete. The owner of the restaurant, Andreas, is a real character, welcoming everyone in from the street and, once people are seated, offering them a raki in the true form of Cretan hospitality. It's a family affair with his son, Dimitrios, helping with the customers and his lovely wife, Stella, supervising the cooking in the kitchen. Andreas makes everyone feel welcome as he rests for a while at each table, sitting to take orders and connecting with people as friends.

"We have everything," he says with a twinkle in his eye, meaning Stella will try to make anything you order or perhaps something close to what you order. They aim to please. Andreas seems genuinely happy to see you in his restaurant and on certain nights, he and Dimitrios stop serving for a while and play traditional Cretan music on their instruments. If you wave to get his attention to get your bill, he will simply wave back to you! If you ask for your bill, he will bring you dessert—melon or grapes or another raki on ice to entice you to stay a little longer.

"Sit and enjoy your dinner, like you would in your own house," says Andreas. Of course, we always choose to stay a little longer!

Unique Spirit

Hospitality involves connecting with the unique spirit of each person. Importantly, it involves taking a genuine interest in the person, versus treating him or her as a transaction or as someone from whom you can gain something. It's saying, "I care about you as an interesting human being," not "This is what you can do for me."

We have stayed at the Aegean Pearl Hotel in Rethymno many times, not only because of the luxurious surroundings, modern amenities, and delicious food but also, most of all, because it feels like our home away from home. A hotel can be just a hotel, a building with beds, but the Aegean Pearl is an experience mainly due to the hospitality of the staff, led by Eugenios Fragiadakis, a true manifestation of the Cretan Greek spirit.

We first met Eugenios early one morning as we observed him going table by table through the dining room, chatting with the guests. We assumed he was asking how they liked the breakfast or if the eggs were cooked to their satisfaction. It wasn't until he stopped by our table that we realized that Eugenios was very special.

"Where will you be going today?" he asked us, connecting in his distinctly humanistic way. We explained that we had heard of a small village in the mountains that we wanted to visit but weren't sure if we knew the correct name. Promptly, Eugenios asked to see our map and proceeded to trace a route for us to the very village we wanted to go to.

Each day we watched Eugenios connect with the other guests and each day he asked us how our travels had been, suggesting new places for us to visit and, of course, recommending that today, as always, would be a good day for a swim in the sea. Eugenios is one of those people who genuinely takes an interest in other people, who honors the unique spirit of each person he meets, and who truly embodies the Greek spirit of hospitality.

The spirit by which someone offers hospitality is important. We all know the signs when someone cares: They look deeply into our eyes and take time to connect with us. They not only talk but listen, and they don't rush the conversation. We feel genuine interest and meaningfully engaged after having had a conversation with them!

At work, it is also important for leaders and managers to see themselves as "hosts" if they really wish to create a more human-centered, meaning-focused workplace. By taking a genuine interest in others, by understanding what is important to them, by enriching them and making them feel stronger with every interaction, members of the team will feel like they belong, that they matter, that their work matters, and that their work can be a source of meaning in their lives.

What you do for others, you do for yourself. One good deed leads to another; favors are returned as well as passed forward. When you share the love, you put love into the universe and, in turn, you share in this universal love. This is the cycle of hospitality that is an integral part of the Greek DNA.

Do a good deed and throw it into the sea.
TRADITIONAL VILLAGE WISDOM

You must give before you can receive. However, many of the Greeks we met were more altruistic in their beliefs about honoring the human spirit through hospitality. They believed in giving something without the expectation of return and without the expectation of any benefit or reward. They were simply sharing what they had, helping others. They gave openly with their hearts and spirits. They believed that the reward of a good deed comes solely from the joy in having done the deed. Indeed, we're sure that Zeus Xenios would be very proud!

Summary

The Greek word philoxenia literally means "love of strangers." So often in our travels across Greece, we experienced random acts of kindness from people who wanted to help us find our way, teach us about the traditional Greek village way of life, or just share whatever they had with us. Through their kindness, generosity, and treatment of each person as a unique human being and spirit and not simply as a transaction, we confirmed that Greeks truly believe that hospitality is in their DNA; it is an integral part of their being.

Many Greeks, both ancient and present-day, have taught us that we will have meaning in our lives if we extend beyond ourselves and open our hearts to give to others without the expectation of return. This self-transcendent principle suggests that, by extending beyond ourselves, we can fulfill or realize *more* of ourselves. This is where the cycle of hospitality truly manifests itself as the cycle of life. Understanding this helps us find more joy and deeper meaning in our lives and, in turn, enables us to truly live The OPA! Way.

OPA! AFFIRMATION

I find joy and meaning in my life when I connect
meaningfully with others through hospitality.

5

Connect with *Honor*

"We should stop by the bakery and get something to bring to Iakovos and Elsa's house," I suggested to Alex, feeling that we shouldn't go empty-handed to our cousins' home, especially in light of their kind hospitality. "Okay, I think I saw a bakery down this way," offered Alex, leading the way down a narrow alley past a small souvenir shop and its overflowing display of embroidered linen tablecloths hanging from the rafters, all gently swaying in the cool evening breeze. We passed a shop that proudly displayed its soft leather shoes, handcrafted in Greece. We passed the pharmacy and the jewelry shop, with its glistening display. Alas, no bakery was in sight.

"Maybe it was this way," suggested Alex, taking a sharp right turn at the next alleyway.

"Maybe we should just ask!" I said, spotting an old man sitting quietly nearby on a rickety old blue chair in front of a leather shop. As we approached him, his kind eyes turned to meet us.

"Where is the bakery?" we asked. He did not reply. The only sound we heard was the quiet clanging of his worry beads as he tossed them slowly back and forth with his left hand. We stood before him, wishing for him to hurry up with his answer, but he just continued to stare, straight into our eyes, straight into our souls. After pondering our question for

what seemed to be a few minutes, he slowly raised his weathered right hand and gestured for us to proceed just around the corner. We thanked him for his efforts and, upon turning the corner, were greeted by the green doors of the old-fashioned bakery we were looking for.

As we have learned so many times in Greece, don't rush the human interaction. Honor the presence of others and show respect for them. The urgency of the task at hand is less important than the quality of the energy that flows between people. There is always time to connect meaningfully with others.

Philotimo

In Greece, there is a very important word and complex concept called "philotimo," derived from the Greek words philos (love) and "timi," which means "honor," that roughly translates to the "love of honor." Considered to be the highest of all Greek virtues, philotimo to the Greeks is essentially a way of life in itself. In this regard, it involves such ideas as loyalty, duty, integrity, being mindful of the sense of right and wrong, and having respect for oneself and others. Philotimo (also spelled filotimo) involves feeling pride for doing the *right* thing and doing things *right*, as well as for honoring and sharing in the pride of others when they act in a similar way.

"Filotimo to the Greek is like breathing. A Greek is not a Greek without it. He might as well not be alive."
—THALES

Respect

The word "honest" comes from the word "honor." To be *honest* means that we are showing great honor to ourselves and to others. It begins with authentically respecting ourselves: respecting our strengths and good deeds; respecting our body; respecting our feelings and emotions; and, on a metaphysical plane, respecting who we truly are as a human being. When we are aligned with our highest self, when we truly respect ourselves, we are able to express ourselves honestly and show the world our authentic self. Respect begins with ourselves and then radiates outward into the world.

We parked our car snugly at the side of the winding road and began our hike down the steep hillside toward the base of the gorge. Having learned not to rush our journey, we stopped to admire the breathtaking view. The majestic peak of Crete's highest mountain, Mount Psiloritis, also known as Mount Ida, stood before us. This mountain holds a very special place in Greek mythology as the place where Zeus was born and raised. As we continued our descent, we remarked to each other how peaceful it was to be in nature. Continuing our conversation, we noticed a slight echo sounding in the valley. "S'agapo (I love you)," we each shouted. The mountain repeated back to us, "S'agapo." We knew at that moment the mountain and Zeus were teaching us something special. Everything we think, say, and do in our lives will come back to us in some manner.

As with our meaningful experience in the shadow of Mount Psiloritis, whatever we put out will be reflected back to us in some way—in our own lives, in our own well-being, and in our relationships with others. (Of interest, the word "echo" comes from the Greek myth of Echo, the nymph who was involved in a failed scheme to seduce Zeus and was punished by the loss of her voice, except to repeat the last words of others.)

Similarly, the Greek expression *gyro gyro* (pronounced *yee-row yee-row*) literally means "around and around."

(Throughout Greece, we saw many gyro machines, which are the vertical rotisseries on which the meat used to make the famous Greek gyro sandwich is held.) The world (universe) is like a giant gyro machine—what goes around comes around. Our thoughts, words, and deeds will return to us in the reflection of thoughts, words, and deeds of others.

As every farmer in every Greek village knows, we get what we sow. If we sow love and honor, we will receive love and honor; by the same token, if we sow hatred and dishonesty, we will receive hatred and dishonesty in return. So if we want more respect in our lives, we need to create more respect in our hearts. If we want to live in better villages or neighborhoods, or work in better workplaces, we must do our part first to create these conditions. Honor and respect are closely interrelated; together they form the basis necessary for connecting meaningfully with others.

Respecting Others

The word "dialogue" comes from the Greek words "dia," meaning "passing through," and "logos," roughly translated in English as "reason," "sense," or, as we are using it, "meaning." On one level, then, dialogue refers to the interpersonal process of arriving at a common understanding—that is, a shared meaning, of something. Upon closer examination, however, the various translations of the common Greek word logos reveal also that it has deep spiritual roots. In fact, one of the first references to logos as "spirit" came from the ancient Greek philosopher Heraclitus around 500 BC. Against this backdrop, the process of dialogue takes on a new and deeper meaning when it is perceived as "shared spirit" rather than just shared meaning. Authentic dialogue, in other words, enables individuals to access a pool of common spirit through a genuine and meaningful connection with others. Moreover, it enables individuals to acknowledge honestly and respect-fully that each is part of a greater whole, that they naturally resonate with others within this whole, and that the whole is indeed greater than the sum of its various parts.

In true dialogue, the conversation between people is open and authentic, demonstrating that mutual respect (even when there are differences of opinion), civility, and accepted rules of engagement guide the process. It is im-portant to underscore that with every dialogue, in fact with every conversation, we either strengthen or weaken our relationships; we either honor or dishonor others. Unlike other forms of interpersonal communication, such as dis-cussions and chats, real dialogue, by definition, is grounded in conversation that meaningfully connects people by show-ing respect for one another's presence (body), contributions (mind), and importantly, spirit. It seeks to create a space of psychological safety in which people really can say what they mean and mean what they say. Encouraging people to communicate in such an authentic and transparent way, of course, is not always easy; however, it is necessary if we expect to connect meaningfully with others.

Our good friend Mathew wisely told us, "You must be very careful with your words. Only use words you really mean. They must come from your heart. If you say good morning to someone, really mean it. If you say *s'agapo* (I love you), really mean it." This sentiment was echoed by Panos, our taxi driver, who shared his views on the state of today's conversations: "Today, the conversations seem so superficial. We see others' lips moving but they aren't saying what's in their hearts . . . and we've replaced real conversations with sound bites, texting, and wearing ear-phones so that no one is really connecting. We also talk too much about things that don't matter and not enough about things that do."

Respecting others means that we are truly interested in them as real people, and that we're not simply interested in them for their titles, fame, money, or possessions. Respecting others means we respect people for who they are and don't always see them as a means to an end, or want them to do things for us. Having respect for others is especially important in today's workplace, where interpersonal communication tends to be not only more complex and multifaceted but also more superficial and impersonal due to the paradoxical influence of *high-tech* but not necessarily *high-touch* technologies.

Many people feel disengaged from their work and one of the main causes is the lack of respect and appreciation shown by coworkers for their opinions, ideas, and contributions. On a human level, everyone wants to know that their voice is heard, that they are valued and not overlooked, and that their efforts really matter. Leaders can inspire people simply by helping them feel respected and involved. In many circumstances, respect, appreciation, a sense of belonging, and acceptance are more important motivations than the paycheck is. This fact of life makes it especially important for us to connect with honor and, in turn, to connect meaningfully with others both during and away from work. As we know, gyro gyro—if we want respect, we have to give respect.

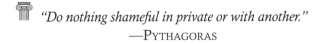 *"Do nothing shameful in private or with another."*
—PYTHAGORAS

Engaging in "good" behavior involves showing respect to ourselves, parents, family, friends, neighbors, other *villagers*, and even strangers, while engaging in "bad" behavior, in its various forms, is essentially showing disrespect and dishonor to all those around us. We found in Greece that everyone's actions affect the reputation of the family and village, so everyone is ultimately responsible for maintaining and living by a code of honor. This results in a type of social self-regulation where everyone is expected to be mindful of their actions to and in relation with others, thereby increasing their feelings of connection. "What will people say?" is an expression we hear often that reflects the pressure to live up to family and village expectations and standards: appearances matter, doing well matters, being considerate of others matters.

In practical terms, we have found that in places where people closely adhere to the concept of philotimo, such as in the traditional villages and smaller towns where primary relationships between residents are still the norm, the need for any form of law enforcement is virtually nonexistent. In effect, it would be dishonorable and a violation of philotimo to do wrong to someone else or to someone else's property. The virtue of philotimo, in other words, acts as a deterrent to criminal behavior.

The word "crime" derives originally from the Greek word "krima," which actually means "shame." Again, we heard variations of the following message many times by Greeks we encountered, even during the crisis, "There is no need to worry. We have low crime here," meaning that the people in the village or town were honorable and would not do anything shameful. People feel valued so they act with honor. They show respect for others and for their goods and property. Throughout our travels across Greece, we witnessed many tavernas where the furniture was left in place outside, overnight, and not chained to avoid theft, as we have seen in other places around the world.

Traditionally, acts of violence and crime were unacceptable because they ran counter to the Greek notion of honor. Even protests against government policies were focused on the principle of democracy and were designed to allow the opportunity for citizens to voice opposition to a policy without resorting to violent acts. Of course, in the larger metropolitan areas that have been hard hit by austerity measures imposed during the economic crisis, the concept of philotimo has been put to the test. Typically, most of the protests in Greece have remained peaceful. However, when people don't feel respected or valued, they frequently respond by acting disrespectful and value*less*, which, in turn, has a negative effect on the whole "village."

Meeting human needs during such challenging times requires much more focus and reliance on philotimo, not less. We believe that by connecting with honor, by restoring the virtue of philotimo, and by demonstrating respect for others, the expression of anger and frustration through violence, be it in the home, in the traditional Greek village, in the metropolis, in the public square, or in the workplace, can be lessened or avoided. At the very same time, by practicing these "rules of *meaningful* engagement," potentially violent forms of expression can be replaced by civil discourse, enhanced understanding, and heightened awareness of interdependency between the stakeholders seeking a resolution to their differences. In short, an authentic commitment to the ethical value of respect is a prerequisite for connecting meaningfully with others. When Greeks rediscover and return to their cultural roots, we have no doubt that this highest of virtues will once again take center stage, demonstrating to the world that the concept of philotimo is alive and well.

Respecting Traditions

There is also great meaning in respecting traditions that weave the village together in a common bond. Passing on the traditions to the next generation ensures continuity and respect for the old ways. Rituals are good for the soul whether they involve meeting with friends at the same kafenio each day; participating in ceremonies, such as weddings, that mark the milestones of life; or partaking in public affairs, such as voting in elections.

Pride in one's heritage and family history is shown in the tradition of naming children after relatives, which, among other things, helps everyone to remember that the ancestor's spirits live on to guide generations to come. The birth of the first child is a major event as it represents that the family and family history will continue on. It is tradition for the first son to be named after the paternal grandfather, or *pappou*, and the first daughter to be named after the maternal grandmother, or *yiayia*. Being able to say, "My name is Nicholas, my grandfather's name is Nicholas, and his grandfather's name was Nicholas," shows an understanding of the history of the family and reinforces the strong bonds with the past. Like a thread weaving through the ages, understanding your ancestral roots helps you understand yourself. During our travels we had a wonderful evening with Giorgos and Maria Protodakis, reviewing our extensive family tree, encompassing six or seven generations, and still a work in progress! Beaming with enthusiasm, cousin Giorgos exclaimed that the Pattakos family is a very big and proud family!

As many yiayias told us, "Never forget your roots; never forget where you came from." In the villages of Greece, elders are respected for their wisdom and as mentors who bring out the best in others. We frequently saw three or four generations eating dinner together, interacting and sharing in the activities of life. While visiting YiaYia Maria, we witnessed her gifting baby blankets she had knitted to her young grandchildren, so that one day, perhaps twenty years from now, when they have children, they will have treasures from their great grandmother.

"We ought not to treat living creatures as shoes or household belongings, which when worn with use we throw away."

—PLUTARCH

In turn, there is an obligation to take care of the elderly, a concept called "gerotrophia," which literally means feeding the old. In the spirit of honor, you are viewed as not a good person and not a good member of the village if you do not. Unfortunately, in many postmodern societies, the elderly are no longer valued, let alone prized, for their experience and wisdom. Instead, these cultures tend to overvalue youth and undervalue elders, overvalue knowledge and undervalue wisdom. The young may have always thought they knew more than their elders, but unfortunately this divide is even more evident today with the advent of the internet, where *instant* knowledge is readily available. But we must all remember that there is a big and *meaningful* difference between knowledge acquired from the internet and deep wisdom gained from life's experiences! "There are no experienced young people. Time makes experience," wisely observed Aristotle.

Elders typically have a different view of the world: they see things longer term with the obvious benefit of hindsight tempered by experience, they believe in the value of lasting interpersonal and face-to-face relationships, and they cherish time and things that last. Young people, on the other hand, typically view life short term; they are in a hurry and see things as replaceable. As YiaYia Maria says, "The young people are always asking, 'What time is it? What time is it?'" as they are impatient to finish their visit and get back to their friends and activities.

We had to smile one day when we were explaining the tradition of the New Year's Day bread or cake, called the "vasilopita," to a young boy in America. The ritual is to slice the cake and give the slices to participants in order of age from eldest to youngest. A coin is hidden inside the cake, which brings good luck for the year to whoever receives it in their slice. "But then what happens?" asked the young boy, "What do they get?"

"The coin," we answered.

"Just a coin?" he asked, with a disappointed look on his face. (Perhaps he wished to trade in the coin for an iPhone or something of seemingly greater material value, we thought!)

Another way that villagers connect across generations and with other living members of the village is through the celebration of "name days." On these days, all people who share the same name celebrate life and its ultimate meaning as it pertains to relationships with others. According to the Greek Orthodox Church, the prevailing religion in Greece, every day of the year is dedicated to the memory of at least one saint or martyr; so, if someone is named after one of them, then there is a big celebration on his or her "name day." We celebrated our cousin Giorgos' name day with friends and family, all gathered around a long table covered with platters of wonderful food. As we looked around the Taverna Tou Zeze, we saw many other groups celebrating the name day of Giorgos at the very same time! As there are many common names in Greece, such as Nicholas, Giorgos, Yannis, Maria, Eleni, etc., there are many celebrations on these respective name days, each crossing the generational divide in ways that we don't often see in America. (If you happen to have a unique name, or one that may not be associated with a Christian saint by the same name, you can still celebrate your name day on a special day called All Saints' Day.)

The emphasis of name day celebrations is to wish the celebrants a positive, that is, happy, healthy, and meaningful future, so you'll hear common phrases such as "Chronia Polla" (may you live many years) and "na ta ekatostisis" (may you live to be a hundred). This is opposite to how we typically celebrate birthdays, when we focus on the past and observe the number of years completed.

Deceased members of the village are remembered during funerals and ceremonies that occur nine days, forty days, six months, a year, three years, and five years after the person's passing. These meaning-focused rituals, including the lighting of candles, help to honor their spirits and keep the connection with them strong over time. There is also a tradition of wearing black for three years out of respect for a dead relative or close friend. Because the elderly have many relatives and friends who have passed on, they tend to wear black a lot, sometimes for the rest of their lives.

Respecting Nature

One day while wandering through a Greek town, we noticed an old lady sitting outside on an old chair, enjoying the fresh morning air. As we got a little closer to her, we noticed her sweater. It was old, well-worn and, of course, black. But as we looked a little closer, we noticed one brown button on the sweater, obviously replacing a lost black button. We thought, "When was the last time we sewed a button on a piece of clothing?"

We reflected on our "throwaway society," where we tend to toss any item that supposedly has had its day into the garbage, where it might sit in a landfill for generations, and simply replace it with a new one. Not so in the villages in Greece! Here, everything has value. Nothing is wasted. Greek villagers think of the consequences of throwing things into the garbage and how that impacts the environment. If an item could have some remaining value, why not continue to use it instead of creating large mountains of garbage?

This practical view of consumption respectfully builds on the long-standing Greek tradition of olive production—*every part of the olive tree is used*. The olives are used for eating and for making olive oil, soap, and cosmetics. The olive pits and slush from the crushed olives are used for fertilizer and to heat the home, and the leaves are used for bedding and for the traditional Olympic celebration wreath or "kotinos."

Respect on a human level extends to respect for nature, an ecosystem shared by all. The Greeks we've met are deeply connected to their environment—the animals, plants, rivers, land, and earth. (In Greek mythology, Gaia was the primordial earth goddess, also known as "Mother Nature" or "Earth Mother.") They understand how to nurture and take care of this relationship. Indeed, many times we heard villagers call the land the "edible landscape." Living in harmony with and connected to the land, they know that the decisions they make today about how they treat the land will affect generations to come. Unlike some who are focused on maximizing their returns by taking all they can get, without regard for nature or the next generation, the Greeks we met in the villages took only what they needed and left the rest. They had overcome the desire for more and more. They were "green" well before it was trendy to be green!

We can all follow their lead and become more "green" in how we relate to the land, both individually and collectively. The lack of genuine concern for the environment, which is reflected in such things as the packaging used for products, the amount of garbage and pollution generated, and the reliance on genetically modified or altered native plants and animals, are all issues that must be addressed if we are to truly honor and respect nature, the environment, and the whole ecosystem that unconditionally connects and sustains us all.

Friendship

In today's busy world, many people are more likely to tell their hopes and troubles to bartenders, taxi drivers, hair stylists, and therapists rather than be truly honest with the people who are regularly in their lives. Many people have drifted away from the village concept and are now living very private, even lonely, lives. Despite connecting with new friends online, despite living in cities among thousands of people, and despite working in large organizations, the incidence of people who say they are *lonely* keeps rising.

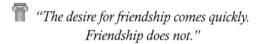 *"The desire for friendship comes quickly.*
Friendship does not."

"A friend to all is a friend to none."

"A friend is a single soul dwelling in two bodies."
—ARISTOTLE

To reduce loneliness, it is better to have one wise friend than many distant ones. Socrates believed that there is no possession more valuable than a good and faithful friend. Aristotle believed that good friends were superior to any material possessions one might have. He also believed that it takes time and effort to build true friendships where you share private thoughts and reveal more of yourself. Through authentic dialogue and activity with others, we become more *of* ourselves, we discover new sides of ourselves, and, not surprisingly, we also are able to find new sides of others. A true friend has the courage to say what needs to be said, even if not always what we may want to hear, to help us grow into our full selves and reach our highest potential.

*"There are only two people who can tell you the truth
about yourself—an enemy who has lost his temper
and a friend who loves you dearly."*
—Antisthenes

"In giving advice, seek to help, not to please, your friend."
—Solon

Finding meaning in our life is up to *us* but we shouldn't underestimate the impact or influence that others can have on our well-being, self-esteem, motivation, and ultimate success. Importantly, we must be more aware of who is supporting our highest good as opposed to who is not. It is best to minimize time spent with people who drown our dreams, withhold approval, belittle or disrespect us, or who take away our strength. If we find we are sacrificing our own needs for the sake of keeping a relationship going, or that we can't have an open, honest conversation with the other person, we may need to admit the relationship is no longer working. If others are not treating us with respect and the relationship is not based on honor, we need to move on; otherwise, we will find ourselves relying on "other esteem" rather than building "self-esteem." In addition, we must reflect on whether *we*, in turn, are being a positive or negative influence on others and whether or not we are being a good friend to others.

*"The key is to keep company only with people who
uplift you, whose presence calls forth your best."*
—Epictetus

Good friends are generous and bring joy and meaning to our lives. Good friends give us energy. Good friends give us a sense of security in our rapidly changing world. When all is said and done, it is best to spend our time with people who inspire us and who support our personal search for meaning.

"People are like dirt. They can either nourish you and help you grow as a person or they can stunt your growth and make you wilt and die."
—PLATO

Connecting with other inspirational people improves our health and well-being, and helps us discover deeper meaning in our lives. Real friendship is like a warm blanket that wraps itself around our soul. Our Greek cousins Iakovos and Elsa, who are also dear friends, exemplify this kind of spiritual energy—love radiates from their hearts as they embrace us with their friendship, a true manifestation of connecting meaningfully with others.

Interestingly, Pythagoras believed in the concept of reincarnation, that the soul of a person comes back to Earth to live another life and continue the journey to enlightenment. Against this backdrop, he also believed that we should love *all* people because we never know if they may have been one of our friends in a previous life!

Compassion

Difficult times show us who our true friends are. As Epicurus professed, "It is not so much the help of a friend but the confidence of their help." The confidence that they will be there for us and that they are partners with us on all parts of our journey, is grounding and helps us navigate through the fog of life's many formidable challenges.

In Greece, friends stick together, families stick together, especially in difficult times or during periods when they are threatened by outside forces. Sometimes, those outside forces are simply other members of the village or of neighboring villages. There is an understanding: "If you insult any members of my family, I will view it as an insult to me and take it personally." Sometimes the family comes before the village. Family-based feuds within and between villages are not unexpected in Greece. Not everyone practices the art of forgiveness with their neighbors despite it being highly recommended by the elders and the ancient Greek philosophers!

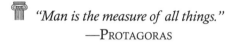 *"Man is the measure of all things."*
—Protagoras

Conflict is part of life. Although we may wish it to be different, every encounter, every interaction presents a chance for conflict because others may see the world differently than we see it. The pre-Socratic Greek philosopher Protagoras believed that "what seems true to each man is true" and "man is the measure of all things." This laid the foundation for our modern thought that perception is reality. Truth, in other words, is relative since each person views a situation from his or her own vantage point, based on individual experiences and beliefs. To believe that there will be no conflict in our lives is naïve and, in many ways, dangerous (remember the meaning of OPA!, spelled with an omega, ΩΠΑ, as described in chapter two).

You cannot connect meaningfully with others if you believe that you have a monopoly on truth.

Conflict frequently arises when we believe the world should operate according to our expectations and that we should have some control over what others think, say, or do. Conflict arises when we believe our way is the best, or even, the *only* way. Conflict also can arise when we react negatively to what others say and do. We feel the world isn't fair and we want to restore fairness, or at least our vision of what constitutes fairness, to the world. We feel that others are not honoring us; they are not treating us the way we want to be treated. We feel that we are a victim of their unjust actions or words.

We can react to this conflict by fighting, freezing, or fleeing. Regardless of our chosen response, stress will be a result, whether we *fight* using words or actions, *freeze* and do nothing in an attempt to sweep the conflict "under the rug," or *flee* or withdraw without resolving or bringing closure to the situation. If we experience any of these scenarios, subconsciously if not consciously, we are effectively choosing to resist "what is." In other words, we are making a decision to resist what actually happened and to resist—by trying in vain either to ignore or marginalize—who the other person really is. Paradoxically, these kinds of strategies seldom achieve the results intended and often backfire, especially when the stress remains due to unresolved conflicts and issues. In this regard, fighting, freezing, and fleeing, more often than not, result in giving your power away rather than finding a balance of power, including compromise, which can be used to achieve reconciliation.

To make matters worse, our conflicts, both real and perceived, can be amplified when emotions are triggered within us that stem from events or situations in our past that remain unresolved. We may be more sensitive, even *hyper*sensitive, and overreact if the recent event reminds us of an earlier time when someone had dishonored us. Again, under the present circumstances, we may feel that we are not being honored and, as a result, want desperately to separate and protect ourselves from further emotional injury. The bottom line, whatever we *do*, is that ultimately it comes down to a *choice* that we, and only we, can make. As the late Stephen Covey wisely espoused in his foreword to our book, *Prisoners of Our Thoughts*, "Between stimulus and response, there is a space. In that space lies our freedom and our power to choose our response. In our response lies our growth and our happiness."

In traditional Greek village life, there is a proverb, "anger takes out your eyes," meaning anger blurs our vision; it blinds us so that we can see only our side of a situation or the negative in a situation. We are filled with feelings of resentment and hurt, and the more we think about the situation, the angrier we become. We know we are right. We spend time and effort trying to justify our position and get others, who may not even be involved in the conflict, to agree with us. We want the other person or persons (or the village or organization) to acknowledge that we were right and they were wrong in their unjust treatment of us. We may even be consumed with thoughts of revenge and of "evening the score"; we want others to suffer because we have suffered.

> *"Whoever grows angry amid troubles applies a drug worse than the disease."*
> —SOPHOCLES

Although we are frustrated and continue to suffer from our anger, on some level we feel the need to stay in it in order to justify our position. When we spend our time and energy in anger and resistance, we become stuck or, as we've written before, we become "prisoners of our thoughts." Our energy becomes frozen and ceases to flow freely. We become trapped emotionally and this starts to take a toll on our health—in body, mind, and spirit. Soon we can't sleep, we can't concentrate, we get tired, and our physical bodies begin to hurt under the heavy weight of the anger that we have *chosen* to carry. Life is about energy and when we resist what *is*, failing to forgive, we store negative energy in our minds and bodies. When we choose to remain angry, we are choosing to block the energy flow in our bodies as well as in our minds and spirits and, in the final analysis, we are *choosing* to make ourselves sick. We have met the true "enemy" involved in our conflict, and whether we want to admit it or not, ironically it is us!

Forgiveness

Anger is reactive. Forgiveness is proactive. Forgiveness means letting go of our own suffering. If we hold on to our suffering, we are unable to let life flow through us. If we hang on to feelings of anger, hurt, or resentment, or if we feel that we are a victim of our circumstances, we essentially are admitting that we did not have a choice about how we responded to whatever might have happened. Focusing our attention on someone else's guilt only serves to continue our own pain and, in effect, imprison our soul. We will never be fully at peace with ourselves, let alone with someone else, unless we let go of our suffering. In the end, forgiveness actually has much more to do with our own health and well-being than with that of the other person or persons we forgive.

 "You can knock all you want at a deaf man's door."
—NIKOS KAZANTZAKIS, from *Zorba the Greek*

We may be waiting for the other person to hear our complaints and acknowledge that we are "at his or her door," waiting for an apology. We think that this will make us feel better. But we shouldn't wait for others to make the first move—they may never be aware of our concerns or, worse yet, may never want to change. In either case, we need to realize that they are "deaf" to our knocking at their door, so we'll be waiting forever for something that will never arrive! Moreover, waiting for others in this way makes the process of our healing dependent on them, not on us. Again, we must try not to get stuck and become a prisoner of our thoughts by saying, "When they do x, then I will forgive them."

 *"Waste not fresh tears over old griefs."*
—EURIPIDES

Instead of wasting precious time and energy carrying around negative thoughts, which are then reflected in our words and actions and are harmful to our bodies, we can simply choose to start the process of forgiving. The act of for*giving* involves *giving* to others: giving others our blessings and relief from our anger and resentment. We will know that we have reached this stage when we are no longer negatively influenced by their presence or have adverse reactions to hearing their names or seeing them. In other words, the tension and drama finally end. We will have regained control of our emotions and started to heal ourselves. We will have released them from our anger and, with authenticity and transparency, wished them the best in life. Like water flowing over rocks, we are in a state of nonresistance; we are no longer resisting what is. We don't have to agree with what has happened, nor do we have to condone the misdeed, but we do need to gracefully accept the situation, surrender to it, and ultimately let it go. We need to release ourselves and others so we can all move forward, ideally learning and growing from the experience so that we may avoid a similar situation from happening in the future.

In Greek mythology, the new city of Athens was to be granted to the god who offered the best gift for humanity. Poseidon offered a freshwater spring. Although this was well received, it was Athena who offered what they deemed to be the best gift—the sacred olive tree. A branch from the olive tree symbolizes peace and goodwill. Wreaths made from the olive branches were worn by brides at their wedding as well as by victors at the ancient Olympic Games. (The olive branch also symbolized peaceful times, when all wars stopped for the duration of the Games.) Many nations' flags, as well as the seal of the United Nations, now feature olive branches in their designs. Today, we use the term "extending an olive branch" to refer to extending an offer of peace and friendship.

Following this line of reasoning, when we have a conflict with someone and don't know where to begin to resolve it, we could find or make something and take it to the other person as a gesture, symbolizing the olive branch of peace. On the one hand, this simple-sounding move, when made with integrity, helps us release them from our anger; on the other hand, it demonstrates to the other person that we are willing to seek reconciliation through forgiveness. In this way, we let go of our resentment and move past what *should have been* to what *is*.

Honoring Compassion

"Be kind, for everyone you meet is fighting a hard battle."
—PLATO

People's lives are far more complicated than they appear to be on the outside. We never really know all the struggles someone else may be facing. And as we know from every Greek tragedy, every person has strengths and weaknesses, good qualities and not-so-good qualities! We must not make assumptions about what others are thinking, jump to conclusions about their positions on issues, or assume that we know how they are feeling at any specific point in time. We need, instead, the courage to have *authentic* conversations with them, to ask them the questions we need to ask rather than sweep things under the rug for the sake of convenience or other reasons.

To forgive is one of the most difficult and challenging things that we can do. However, forgiveness still involves an element of judgment because we are essentially releasing others from what *they* did "wrong." Ultimately, we must move to a higher level of compassion, where we go *beyond* ourselves to seek deep awareness of the suffering of the other person(s) and then, working together, help them relieve both their suffering and our own. This is the only way to show respect and truly honor the other person as well as ourselves. True compassion, in other words, requires that we go to a *higher* ground in order to find *common* ground with those who need more than our forgiveness.

Compassion becomes a higher level of forgiveness because there is no judgment involved.

The word "empathy" is derived from the Greek word "pathos," which, in its most basic sense, means "pain" or "suffering." To have empathy, in this context, means having the capacity for deep understanding of the pain and suffering of others. Empathy is the ability to connect with and honor others—to be able to walk in their shoes, to understand their challenges, to see life from their perspective, to resonate with their feelings, and to understand why they do what they do. Importantly, empathy flows from a state of being nonjudgmental.

We can begin to extend empathy and compassion to others by understanding that they may have different values than we do; they may perceive the world differently and value different things. We are not going to change what they value in life—only they can do this by and for themselves. Our role is to focus less on trying to change others and more on trying to understand them, keeping in mind that there is more than one view of the world that can be "right."

We must trust that others do not really mean to harm us because, under the surface, they may be caught up in their own issues. They may be doing the best they can under the circumstances. They may be caught up in a vicious cycle where someone treated them badly, and now, consciously or not, they treat others badly too. They may be affected by their own fears: fear of losing control, fear of judgment, fear of change, fear of the unknown—any or all of which may become too stressful for them.

When we understand what issues, including fears, others are facing, conflict becomes less threatening to us, and we can have the capacity to focus on *what's right* with a person rather than just on *what's wrong*. We also gain the capacity to acknowledge the humanity that exists within each of us, and we can focus on the things that connect, not divide, us. In the final analysis, having compassion means we open our hearts, and in turn, the world reciprocates by opening up to us.

Some people may be unwilling to discuss their conflict with us. If they refuse to do so, they are telling us that they do not want to have an authentic and transparent relationship with us. In effect, they are not honoring us. We may need to move on.

Others may have been cruel to us. Although it is obviously easier said than done, for our own well-being, we must not take their anger personally. In truth, their words and actions are a reflection of them, not us. They may be emotionally unavailable, perhaps even emotionally un-stable, and may have other issues that are not related to their relationship with us. Again, we can have compassion for their pain, but we can also limit the time we choose to spend with them. We can wish them all the best and freely give them our love and blessings without having to continue to be in their presence. To do otherwise could be interpreted as a form of self-abuse since, in most cases, we retain the option to exercise our freedom of will.

Many of the ancient Greek philosophers believed that it is important for us to realize what we can change and what we cannot. A large part of having compassion for others comes from allowing them to pursue their own journeys without trying to change or influence them.

> *"Do not attempt to heal others when you yourself are full of wounds."*
> —EURIPIDES

> *"You will become a teacher of yourself when for the same things that you blame others, you also blame yourself."*
> —DIOGENES

> *"If you wish to lead the best and most blameless life, refrain from doing that which you blame in others."*
> —THALES

There are many wise quotes from the ancient Greek philosophers that suggest we might see the faults of others but are often blind to our own faults. This was reinforced by Greek villagers who told us that "a donkey cannot see its own load." In honoring both ourselves and others, we should seek to refrain from judging others until we have first gained an awareness of our own words and actions.

Importantly, we need to reflect on what role our words or actions may have played in causing a conflict, such as over-reacting to a situation and inadvertently flaming the fire.

An important element of honor is to forgive *ourselves* for our mistakes, to release the past and move forward. Ironically, nobody tends to judge us as much as we tend to judge ourselves.

Summary

Philotimo, or love of honor, begins with honoring ourselves and then honoring others, traditions, and nature. Honor is reflective, like the law of attraction; how we honor and respect others through our thoughts, words, and actions is reflected back into our own lives. Hence, we must intend to treat others how we, ourselves, would like to be treated.

Our friendships with others are our foundation that can provide pathways to meaning. Among other things, these friendships give us a sense of security and belonging in our lives. Unfortunately, with all relationships comes conflict. To deny that there won't be any conflict in our lives is naïve and potentially dangerous. In the event of a conflict, instead of wasting our energy on anger and sabotaging our own health, prosperity, and success, we should focus our energy in a positive and meaningful direction and leverage it to help us move from anger to forgiveness to compassion. The ability to feel compassion is the highest level in this process, since it involves trying to understand and feel empathy for those who have seemingly done us wrong, as well as helps us to further a deeper understanding of ourselves. Our capacity for compassion provides a pathway to true freedom and self-empowerment that can also be a platform for finding more joy and meaning in our lives. In truth, we cannot reach life's deeper meaning without experiencing forgiveness and compassion for ourselves and others.

Every person we encounter and every event we experience can teach us about meaning. By reaching out to others in the *village*, by providing them with *hospitality*, and by *honoring* them, we can connect authentically with something much larger than ourselves. In doing so, we discover that we matter, that we are part of something special, and that our lives do, indeed, have meaning. OPA!

OPA! AFFIRMATION

I find joy and meaning in my life when I connect meaningfully with and honor others.

Part Three

PURPOSE (P):
Engage with Deeper Purpose

6

Engage with *"Know Thyself"*

One day while vacationing on the beautiful Greek island of Rhodes, a businessman named Howard decided he wanted to go for a little spin on a boat. Down at the docks, Howard ran into Stavros, a proud Greek fisherman who owned a tiny blue and white fishing boat. Howard offered Stavros a few euros to take him around the bay. Although Stavros was technically done for the day, he wanted to share his beautiful island with the tourist, so he complied. As Stavros concentrated on maneuvering his tiny boat around the dock walls into the bay, the silence was broken by Howard.

"How much do you make a week from your catch?" he asked.

Stavros found the question both interesting and confusing. "Enough," replied Stavros. "Enough to feed my family, repair my boat, and save a little for the future."

"Why don't you buy a larger boat with your savings or even a few more boats and catch more fish? You could make five or seven times more, depending on how efficient you are," suggested Howard, thinking he was doing the fisherman a favor by offering free business advice. "After all, bigger is better," continued Howard.

"One boat is enough," Stavros replied. "Besides, it gives me time to spend with my family and friends."

Not one to let go of a good idea, Howard persisted. "But with several boats and a larger catch each day, you could *build a large company and then sell the whole company one day for a large profit."*

"And then what?" asked Stavros.

"Well, then, you can retire in style!" replied Howard enthusiastically.

"Umm, and then what—live in a Greek village, go fishing on a tiny boat in the Mediterranean, and enjoy spending time with my family and friends?" continued Stavros with a sly smile on his tanned and weather-beaten face, as he reached over and gently patted the name so aptly inscribed on the side of his boat: ΓΝΩΘΙ ΣΑΥΤΟΝ (Know Thyself).[1]

The famous Greek saying, *"know thyself,"* is inscribed on a plaque above the entrance to the Temple of Apollo at Delphi, Greece, and is attributed to several Greek philosophers, including Thales, Chilon, Heraclitus, Pythagoras, and most commonly, Socrates. The Oracle at Delphi was an important shrine in Greece where the ancient Greeks came to seek guidance. Their questions were answered by Pythia, the priestess of the Greek god Apollo, but her answers were usually cryptic and open to interpretation.

Once the visitor received an answer from Pythia, the challenge then became deciding what to do with the answer. Should he blindly follow her advice, believing he had received "the answer," or was the inscription *"know thyself"* a warning to decide the validity of the answer for oneself?

The philosophers believed the purpose of the Oracle was to encourage reflection and the use of one's own reasoning and intuition (sense of "inner knowing") to gain further insight into problems. However, Plato believed that, in

---

[1] This story was adapted from the well-known "Fisherman" story—original source unknown.

many situations, we do not need to ask anyone for guidance because we already "know" what the right answer is for us.

"To know thyself is our greatest challenge."
—PLATO

The most difficult thing in life is to "know thyself," that is, to know *yourself*. It takes time and effort—to really question, reflect, and know authentically *who* we are, not what other people want us to be. It takes time and effort to know our strengths and talents, and then to use them in service to others. It also takes time and effort to know our weaknesses and shortcomings, and then to compensate for them so that they don't become excuses for not living a meaningful life. Knowing yourself, to be sure, poses life's most formidable existential challenge, and many of us don't want to "go there," because it demands such hard work and we are either uncertain or afraid of what we may discover about ourselves. However, the human quest for meaning requires that we do accept this challenge and, like Theseus, enter the labyrinth that is our life; it is a sacred path of individuality, and no one can walk it but us.

"Applicants for wisdom, do what I have done:
Inquire within."
—HERACLITUS

In his speech to defend himself at his trial (in *The Apology*), Socrates described how he would go *within*, like Heraclitus, and listen to his inner voice as a means to discover what the "right" thing to do was. His approach was clearly metaphysical; he combined logic and reason with intuition, consulting what we refer to as his "inner oracle." Like Socrates, the challenge for many of us becomes whether we will trust our inner oracle, our sense of inner knowing, or allow ourselves to be swayed by others.

Through observation, questioning, logic, and an understanding of metaphysics, we can change our perspectives and gain greater awareness about "knowing ourselves." The better we understand ourselves, the easier it will be to navigate through life's challenges, rather than be tossed around like a small Greek fishing boat in the rough, ever-changing seas of life.

Authenticity

The roots of Ancient Greek theater can be traced back to 550 BC when the citizens of Athens celebrated a festival called the Dionysia, honoring Dionysus, the god of wine and agriculture and the patron god of the Greek stage. Various forms of plays—tragedy, comedy, and satire—were performed in the Theatre of Dionysus and helped distinguish Athens as an important cultural center.

Masks were an essential part of this theater as they enabled the actors to transform into multiple characters and roles. They also worked well to communicate exaggerated facial expressions so that the audience could see, for example, if a character was happy, sad, or upset. Masks also helped men play female characters since only male actors were allowed onstage at that time. The first to wear a mask was Thespis, a Greek writer, from whose name we derived the word "thespian," which is another word for actor.

Just as actors wore masks in the ancient Greek theater, we wear masks in a metaphorical sense, to hide our true selves, thoughts, and emotions. We excel at wearing masks. We fool our friends, colleagues, even our loved ones with the various masks that we wear. More often than not, we avoid expressing who we really are and what we really think because we want to fit in, gain approval, and importantly, try to minimize, if not avoid, conflict. We wear masks to project the impression or illusion of a more "perfect life"— having the right job or occupation, the right car, the right house, the right spouse or partner, the right clothing, and so on. We hide behind labels, titles, and money. Our real identity is covered up by the false identity of our possessions, roles, actions, and words. Our ego traps us in this artificially staged world; often out of our perceived need for acceptance.

 *"Things love to conceal their true nature."*
—HERACLITUS

Some of us wear masks of grandeur while, conversely, others wear very plain masks. We are often hesitant to express ourselves because we are afraid of possible judgment and rejection from others. We wear masks because we fear others will see who we really are. We feel the need to protect ourselves from judgment and emotional assault, fearing we will expose our weaknesses or won't be good enough or won't belong. Typically, men have learned to hide their weaknesses and feelings and instead to act "strong" by constantly projecting an air of confidence. On the other hand, women have been conditioned to hide their strengths, to act sweet, to appear relatively helpless and, in the same vein, nonthreatening. Like the actors on the Greek stage, we all strive to entertain and please the audience; we worry about having the "right" appearance, saying the "right" lines, and receiving the "right" reviews of our performance after the curtain goes down.

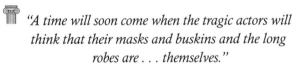

"The worst of all deceptions is self-deception."
—PLATO

The more we wear these masks and play someone else's role, the further away we are from our authentic selves. We lose ourselves when we let others determine who we should be. Swayed by the opinions of others, we lose our own thoughts and start to second-guess ourselves. We ask others what role we should play and what lines we should speak, wishing to conform, trying hard to please them.

We get bullied, in effect, into being someone we are not. When we bow to the audience too often, when we crave their approval, we effectively give the audience—other people—control over us. We empower them by giving away our personal power, and we lose trust and confidence in our inner selves. We are so busy fulfilling the dreams and meeting the expectations of others; and then one day we wake up and ask ourselves the existential question, "Who am I?"

The English words "hypocritical" and "hypocrite" are derived from the Greek words "hypokrisis" (play acting) and "hypokritis" (actor) and refer to the concept of acting, putting on false appearances, or acting in contradiction to our true feelings and beliefs. When we act, when we wear our masks or have a false smile permanently glued to our faces, or when we follow someone else's path rather than our own, we are not living with authenticity. We are not living with meaning.

"A time will soon come when the tragic actors will
think that their masks and buskins and the long
robes are . . . themselves."
—EPICTETUS

As one would expect, there are costs associated with wearing our masks. We struggle more with life when our

92

relationships are not authentic and when we are not even being true to ourselves. Life ceases to flow freely through us and, as a consequence, we grow more and more frustrated, stressed, sick, and depressed. Soon we may simply "burn out." This is why many people view depression as the state of being separated from the true self.

We can continue to wear our masks our whole life, pretending everything is "perfect," or alternatively, there may come a time when we draw a line in the sand, remove our masks, and defiantly say, "This is who I am."

There may come a time when we choose to begin living more authentic, genuine lives—a turning point, or as we call it, an OPA! Moment. In this regard, it took several life-changing experiences, or OPA! Moments (military service, his father's death, divorce, and so forth), for Alex to finally realize that it was time for him to remove his mask. Indeed, removing our masks is a powerful and meaningful symbol of the healing process. This dramatic step serves to illustrate that we are committed to making progress in healing our past dramas and traumas, and that we are now ready to move on, mask-free, to live more authentically.

We know of many people who faced OPA! Moments when they reached a certain age and suddenly realized that it was time to remove their masks and live more honest lives. The incomparable Betty White, an American actress of Greek heritage, is a wonderful example of someone who, now in her nineties, is living a real, high-energy, authentic, and meaningful life. Staying true to form, Betty wisely advised in her book, *If You Ask Me (And of Course You Won't)*, that "You can't get carried away with your image, because you know better than anyone else who the *real* person is."

But what is taking all of us so long to get the message and, most importantly, do something about it? Why are we wearing so many different masks for so many years? To be sure, everyone has different reasons, but one thing we realized is that the people we met in the traditional Greek villages seemed to struggle less with the issue of living authentic lives. Perhaps their true selves aren't so covered up with material goods. Perhaps they feel more accepted by others in their village and therefore feel freer to be who they are . . . Perhaps they know themselves better than we tend to know ourselves.

"Knowing yourself is the beginning of all wisdom."
—ARISTOTLE

Core Essence

In nature, things do not copy another's path—they change and evolve into what they alone are supposed to be. A baby bird learns to fly and becomes an adult bird following its own developmental path. It does not attempt to become a goat. An olive tree can grow and shed its olives but it is still an olive tree. It is not an orange tree. This is the concept of essence or true nature. Every living thing in the world has a natural state and qualities or attributes that make it *who* or *what* it is.

"There is one life for each of us: our own."
—EURIPIDES

Our essence is what defines us and is at the heart of what makes us a unique human being. Although we can belong to a certain group and share characteristics of that group, we are still a unique being with our own unique essence and unique purpose in life. The greatest challenge in life is to discover and embrace our core essence. It is our core essence that frames our sense of self, helps us clarify and understand our purpose, and leads us to more joy and deeper, authentic meaning in life. Many people tend to focus on what type of job or career they think they should have, or how they might define their overall purpose in life, but in actuality, a truly meaningful life starts *from*, remains engaged *with*, and ultimately returns *to* one's core essence . . . awakening our true selves by connecting to who we really *are*.

We can try, of course, to change or hide our essence, say to fit in with the expectations of others, but in the end, we are *who we are* and *who we are meant to be*. We will only find true fulfillment in life if we act in accordance with our core essence. Many people feel depressed because they focus on external rather than internal things and events, work at the outer rather than inner edges of their reason for being, and do not focus on discovering and understanding their *core essence*. If we don't know who we are at the core, or perhaps resist engaging with it, it is more difficult to make meaningful decisions in our lives, and by extension, more difficult to focus our time and energy on our true purpose. Removed from our core essence, we cannot live properly or realize our highest potential. We jump from job to job, relationship to relationship, knowing something isn't right, sensing that there is something else—something more—that we should be doing, but not being able to determine what "right" is. Unfortunately, we are focusing on "what" we are *doing* rather than "who" we *are* and "why" we exist.

"The world turns aside to let any man pass who knows where he is going."
—EPICTETUS

Discovering our true nature, or *core essence*, is part of our natural progression in life and is part of what gives our lives purpose and, ultimately, meaning. Our core essence reveals itself through all of life's experiences, both our joys and our difficulties. Once we understand this basic fact of life, all things become clearer, we come to know and feel more confident about our direction, and we notice that *meaning-focused* energy begins to flow freely to and through us. In other words, we're no longer working against the flow of who we really are. This enables us, instead, to take deliberate steps toward fulfilling our true destiny and achieving our highest potential as human beings.

As a result of rediscovering and staying meaningfully engaged with our core essence, we are better equipped to let go of who we think we should be and stay on the path to becoming who we are meant to be. This powerful life force, in turn, actually radiates outward from us toward others creating, in effect, an energy field of oneness within which everyone feels meaningfully connected. At the same time, we feel in sync with our life and work, so now life and work can resonate with each other and offer deeper sources of meaning than they would have otherwise. We know who we are: We use our talents for our highest good and for the highest good of others; we are energized, passionate, and enthusiastic about our life; and we feel that we are living in harmony with ourselves and the world around us.

The ancient Greeks had a concept, coined by Aristotle, called "entelechia" that described the condition of having fully realized one's essence. In this sense, the notion of entelechia was used to differentiate between potentiality and actuality. It signaled that an ultimate goal of human existence—to achieve our highest potential by becoming who we were actually meant to be—had always been "coded" within us and that the life force or energy needed to realize this *potentiality*—that is, make it an *actuality*—had also been made available to us. As such, our core essence symbolized our innate potential for meaning and fulfillment in life, but it was our personal responsibility to evolve from just having potential to actually realizing our potential and, ultimately, to move ourselves toward this state of entelechia.

The universe will be supportive of our dreams if we are doing what we are meant to do—as in the case of Marianna. One day, during one of our adventures on the back roads in Crete, we stumbled upon the historic village of Maroulas. As we have learned to do in most small villages, we parked our car at the edge of the community and continued our journey on foot. We wandered down a narrow alley past several abandoned buildings, and came upon a tiny shop displaying a wooden sign marked "Marianna's Workshop." We were promptly welcomed in, literally with open arms.

"Come in, come in," Marianna said encouragingly.

We stepped inside the small doorway and before us were several tall wooden racks that held hundreds of small bottles of natural extracts in oil. Our eyes were drawn immediately to the sage and spearmint oils, positioned beside small cellophane bags overflowing with mountain teas.

"For over twenty years, I've been collecting knowledge on herbal living, helping people overcome their health problems using our traditional ways and recipes. I collect the aromatic medicinal herbs from our mountainside, cleanly grown under our Greek sun, and use them to prepare oils and teas," she proclaimed with a great deal of confidence and pride.

We spent the next hour listening intently to Marianna's adventures, learning from her expertise. Her passion for her work was so obvious and contagious. "I love explaining this to you," she said, as she opened jar after jar for us to smell the aromas from the products she and Mother Nature had created. Indeed, Marianna had found purpose in her life and work by following both Nature and her own true nature, her core essence. She discovered that doors opened and life

became easier and, to be sure, more meaningful once she con-
nected with her true nature.

🏛 *"All things will be produced in superior quantity and*
quality, and with greater ease, when each man
works . . . in accordance with his natural gifts."
—PLATO

Aristotle taught that there is a tendency for everything to become what it is meant to be. He used a phrase, "the what it was to be" (translated directly from the Greek), to express the notion of core essence. In other words, our true nature has always been there and through our different experiences, reveals itself slowly and deliberately as we evolve. At any point in life, we will have already experienced and reflected some of our core essence and thus some of our purpose. As spiritual beings having a physical experience, the human quest for meaning can be viewed as a personal odyssey, and much like Odysseus' return to Ithaka, return to our core essence is the final destination.

As we go through life, we begin to realize that we are becoming who we have always been at our core. And as our awareness grows, we begin to realize that we are coming full circle, going back to who we really were in the first place, returning to our roots (before they were covered up with fears and the hardships or dirt of life!).

Like an animal undergoing metamorphosis (derived from the Greek word for transformation), we become who we have always been capable of becoming. We begin to realize that when we achieve something or become something, we always had that potential within us. Only when the conditions become right for this innate potential or possibility to manifest itself, will it morph into an actuality. Just like a seed holds with it the potential to grow into a tree, metaphorically speaking, we have seeds within us that hold our potential to grow into an authentic, meaning-focused human being. Our life, in short, is an ongoing process of personal transformation—bringing forth what is already within us. This is what is meant by realizing our full human potential, or *entelechia*, and importantly, our life's destiny.

In the larger sense, if we believe that our potential to do something already exists—it does exist (in our minds), it is real to us, even though it hasn't happened yet on a physical plane. As our friend Nikos told us one day, during a deep conversation while overlooking the Aegean Sea, "There are two kinds of people in the world: those who believe that the potential already exists and that they will see it later . . . versus those who have to see it first before they will believe it is possible." Fortunately for us, we met many people on our odyssey in Greece whose orientation is "believe first, see later," a trait that is vital for building resilience and dealing with difficult times. This kind of mindset, we found, has been especially important and helpful to many Greeks during the recent financial crisis. Unfortunately, those with the "see first, believe later" orientation are more likely to spend too much time waiting for things to happen and, as a result, miss many opportunities that life has to offer.

How do we become more aware of our true nature and wake up to our core essence and its unlimited potential? As Nikos Kazantzakis once said, "Everything in the world has a hidden meaning." Although it may be much later when we discover and understand the hidden meaning of something that has happened to us, rest assured that we all get hints and signs along the way about our core essence, our purpose, and what we are meant to be and do.

According to Greek mythology, after his son was killed in Athens, Minos, the king of Crete, took revenge by demanding that Athens sacrifice seven young men and seven young maidens. They would be sacrificed to the Minotaur, a creature who was half man and half bull. The Minotaur dwelt at the center of the Cretan Labyrinth, an elaborate mazelike structure with winding passages in which one could easily get confused, lost, and eventually killed by the beast within.

A young Athenian named Theseus volunteered to be among the seven males to be sacrificed to the Minotaur. Upon arriving at the labyrinth, Theseus met Ariadne, the eldest daughter of King Minos. Ariadne fell in love with Theseus. Worried that he would be hurt by the Minotaur and become lost in the labyrinth, she gave him a ball of thread. She told Theseus to unwind the ball of thread as he ventured into the depths of the labyrinth so that, after he killed the Minotaur, he would be able to retrace his path and follow the thread back out of the labyrinth and into her arms.

Today, we talk about "Ariadne's thread" in reference to finding the common thread or idea in a maze of information. There is also a common thread or theme within the complex web of our life experiences that can help us find our core essence and purpose in life.

Finding our own path is part of our life story. As we know, every good story has twists and turns, challenges and struggles, joys and celebrations. We must have faith that if things didn't go well for us in the past, then the situation wasn't right for us or we weren't right for the situation . . . or the situation *was* right for us and it was there to teach us something meaningful about ourselves. We must have *faith* that our lives are unfolding as they should, even if reason sometimes suggests that this is not the case.

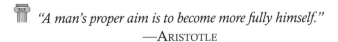 *"A man's proper aim is to become more fully himself."*
—ARISTOTLE

The Greeks believe that with every change, something persists and something new comes into being. Our core essence persists throughout our life but what changes is often our attitudes, surroundings, circumstances, relationships, priorities, and so on. With every change, we are challenged to rethink our core beliefs about who we are and who we are destined to become.

We often fear these life transitions, afraid to leave behind what we know and move into the unknown. We may justify not moving forward by using various excuses, such as lack of time, money, skills, or connections. We may keep our dreams vague or simply say, "I'm stuck, I don't know what to do." We may say that we'll find or return to our true passion when the children grow up or when we've paid off the mortgage. Even though, deep down, we may be discontent with our work and personal life and want something different, that is, something more *meaningful*, we invariably tend to use such excuses to keep "safe" and "secure" within our all-too-familiar comfort zone. In other words, we would rather feel safe than stick out our neck to experience what our authentic self may be "telling" us to do.

We have to be honest with ourselves about what is not working anymore. As we age, we outgrow people, places, and activities. The meaning we attach to these things also changes. We must be willing to let go in order to clear the way for new possibilities to arise. As one Greek fisherman wisely told us, "The tide takes things we no longer need out to sea and the tide brings new things into our lives." Don't fight the tide!

Some of the elders we spoke with both in Greece and in the United States told us that they wished they had been more aware and clear about the meaning of their lives at an earlier age. If only they had been more comfortable with themselves and had let go of some of the beliefs that had limited them, including those about what they could and could not do, they would have found deeper meaning in their lives.

Knowing ourselves is an evolving process. Here are some examples of how we need to know ourselves at various times in our lives:

- As a young adult transitioning into the work world, we need to discover our own path, set out on it, and become responsible for our own successes and failures, no longer reliant on our parents to plan and guide our life. We must believe in the vast potential within each of us and recognize that there are many options—unlimited possibilities—available to us.

- As an unemployed adult, we need to ask ourselves, "Who am I without my job?" We need to get in touch with our true self, not who or what we've been trained to be. We may need to realize that we have grown into a different person than the person who chose a certain line of work in their twenties, and that now is the time to look in a different direction. We may also need to face our new economic reality and make a trade-off by taking a job that may not suit us or offers lower pay. We know that everyone has the ability to contribute in some way and now we must not only find new meaning but also new ways to contribute.

- As someone entering midlife, feeling restless and confused, feeling that we are running out of time, we need to redesign our attitudes toward our present and future life, instead of blindly trying to return to the pleasures of our youth. We need to acknowledge that our future is not solely dependent on our past. Instead, we need to focus on what really matters to us, spend time getting to know our true selves, and take steps to realize our life's destiny by committing authentically to *meaningful* values and goals.

Retirement can also present a Crisis of Meaning. Retirement can be a very difficult time because we are forced to reevaluate who we are and come to grips with such universal issues as the loss of structure and financial security, isolation, health care challenges, and the mistaken perception that "I am what I do." We may wonder what direction to take for the next decade or even think, "What should I do for the rest of my life?" Unfortunately, the current approach to this major life transition is too focused on financial matters, too focused on the question, "Will I have enough money to fund my retirement until I die?" Just because we have saved money for our retirement doesn't mean that we will live a *meaningful* life during the remaining chapters of our lives. Just because we fill our days with activities, no matter how leisurely they may be, it doesn't mean that we will feel fulfilled. Life without purpose and, ultimately, without *meaning*, effectively means that we are dying instead of living.

To retire means to withdraw or retreat. Our perception is that the Greeks we interviewed had an easier time with this transition because their personal identity was rooted in many areas—work, family, the village, social activities, etc.—and not concentrated primarily on their work or occupation. So when one part of a person's life had to be adjusted or removed, his or her "life ship" did not capsize.

The Greeks view aging as a natural process that continues to bring new opportunities. While visiting the island of Santorini, we did what many tourists do; we rode a Greek donkey to the old port! When faced with the prospect of descending the steep stairs from the village of Fira to the water's edge where our boat was waiting, we decided that a donkey ride would be much more interesting and also a little easier than going on foot.

As we approached the row of donkeys leisurely soaking up the Greek sun, an elderly man eagerly motioned for us to choose his two donkeys. His name was Manolis and, at an age when other people might shy away from rigorous activity, he was full of life's energy. It was a happy day for him: The sun was shining, the donkeys were cooperating, and he had a chance to connect with visitors from all over the world.

Manolis proceeded to charm us, caring for us, checking that we were comfortable in the saddles and generally making us feel safe as we descended the steep stairs. He was as sure-footed as the donkeys were and in excellent physical shape from navigating the steep stairs many times as day.

Upon reaching the water's edge, we dismounted, paid his fee, and thanked him again for taking such great care of us. Manolis nodded, grinned from ear to ear, and then quickly turned to lead the donkeys up the stairs to meet his next customer. For Manolis, aging didn't imply that he was weak or no longer of use to others. On the contrary, Manolis found meaning and purpose in every interaction—he felt valued and he felt alive!

Questioning

Thousands of years ago, many Greeks believed that the gods, particularly the goddess of fortune, were responsible for determining who would be successful in life. If someone was not successful, they would blame the gods, holding them responsible for their misfortune. Then along came the Greek philosophers who offered an entirely new perspective: Every man should be responsible for his own life.

"The unexamined life is not worth living."
—SOCRATES

Socrates believed that man was personally responsible for examining and understanding his own life, a basic tenet behind his philosophical argument to "know thyself." He believed that the unexamined life, the life of those who knew nothing of their real selves, aspirations, and actions, was not worthy to be lived because it was devoid of real meaning. The concept of the unexamined *life* also includes the unexamined *relationship*, the unexamined *marriage*, the unexamined *job or career*, the unexamined *retirement*, the unexamined *business* . . . and so forth.

"I know only that I know nothing."
—SOCRATES

The wisest person is the one who is most aware of his or her own ignorance. Socrates stated up front that he "knew nothing" in recognition of his being open to learning new insights. Humbly, he also recognized that there were limits to his knowledge.

*"It is impossible for anyone to begin to learn
that which he thinks he already knows."*
—EPICTETUS

If we are unwilling to ask questions, we are unwilling to learn. Many people are unwilling to do so because they think asking questions, or saying "I don't know," might lessen their power or make them look weak. The opposite is true. Asking questions leads to strength, deeper understanding, and wisdom. The more questions we ask, the more we learn, and the more creative we can become.

It wasn't until we had spent a lot of time in Greece that we understood why the Greeks like to debate so much. In every village and every town we visited, we would see men at the kafenia engaged in what appeared to be rambunctious arguments, with tempers flaring and arms waving madly in the air. We soon came to realize that the desire to discuss and debate issues was in the Greek DNA, going back thousands of years to when Socrates encouraged deep conversations in the agora or marketplace. Through discussion and dialogue with others, we can learn alternative ways of viewing things, but at the same time, we can also learn more about our own opinions and positions when we are forced to support and defend them. Asking deep questions and debating with others are powerful and meaningful parts of the transformational process of knowing yourself.

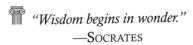 *"Wisdom begins in wonder."*
—SOCRATES

Socrates believed that new insights come when we focus on asking more and deeper questions, instead of rushing to an answer. He also detested superficial answers and suggested we continually ask more and more questions in order to gain deeper insight into the truth behind our assumptions. Many of us aren't aware of the reasons behind what we believe or even feel on an intuitive level. Our beliefs may have simply been passed on to us by or through others, so they are not really our own thoughts. We must think for ourselves and not take the opinions of others to heart without first examining them. And, in some cases, we may need to "unlearn" some of our (limiting) beliefs.

In his Socratic dialogue, The Republic, Plato shares the "Allegory of the Cave" or, as it is commonly known, "Plato's

Cave." In the story, several prisoners are chained for their entire life in a cave facing a blank wall. The only things they can see are shadows projected on the wall. These images shape their reality. They don't question their reality. Then one of them, the philosopher, is freed and once outside the cave, he is able, in the sunlight, to see more and more things. His reality shifts upon experiencing this wider view of things in the bigger world. When he returns to the cave to tell the others, they don't believe him since their world is limited only to the shadows on the wall. The philosopher then has a decision to make: Does he follow his own new knowledge or does he stay with his fellow prisoners in the cave and continue to adhere to their illusions?

It is difficult for us to know ourselves when we are afraid of or avoid asking questions. Perhaps we don't want to acknowledge our illusions or perhaps we don't want to see that we need to change . . . so we just leave it alone, remaining a prisoner of our thoughts in our metaphorical cave. Perhaps we are so busy just running on the treadmill, trying to survive, that we don't want to allocate time to step back and ask the *big* questions . . . or perhaps we are so busy challenging others that we don't make the time to look within and challenge ourselves! Taking time out to think and reflect and to ask the deeper questions, like we do in Greece, is critical to the process of knowing yourself.

Socrates was famous for teaching people *how* to think, not *what* to think. He believed that truth was the highest value and that it could be discovered by examining what we take for granted. He encouraged people to go through a rational and systematic process of questioning their assumptions. Socrates challenged people to give reasons for their beliefs, and if these beliefs did not hold up to rigorous cross-examination, if they were proven false or inconsistent, then he believed these people should be open to considering alternatives and other points of view.

His method, famously referred to as the Socratic Method, is a very dynamic, logical, and analytical process of questioning, examining, and discussing issues of importance, designed to strip away false assumptions and opinions in order to arrive at a higher truth. Socrates recommended that we ask good questions and discuss the various sides of the challenge at hand until new perspectives and ideas surface. In other words, he believed strongly that we shouldn't be trapped into one way of thinking.

New insights and breakthroughs in thinking occur when the original statement or belief is shown to be false. In our experience, when mentoring individuals for both personal and leadership development, as well as when advising clients about innovation management strategies, all too often we've encountered situations where people, albeit with the best intentions, chose simply to ignore these valuable new insights and carry on with their (false) beliefs concerning their personal and work lives instead.

In the face of constant change, some of the beliefs we held yesterday might not fit our lives today. Asking questions helps us understand our thoughts more clearly and provides the clarity and guidance we need to make the right choices for living and working with meaning. This is especially true in Greece where the economic challenges are forcing people to ask new questions about what is really important in their lives and how they choose to live under these new circumstances.

Summary

Life is an odyssey or journey of experiences that teaches us who we really are. Every person we encounter and every event or situation we experience, good or bad, gives us the opportunity to know ourselves better and to know what gives our life meaning. We are all born with our unique, core essence but the choices we make in life can either serve to *conceal* or *reveal* this essence. When we wear "masks," pretending to live someone else's life or trying to "keep up with the Joneses" (or Jonesopouloses), we lose sense of our true selves and, tragically, we disconnect from that part of ourselves that makes us unique. In turn, this affects in negative ways our ability to be comfortable with *who* we are and to connect *meaningfully* with others.

When we ask more questions and examine our lives like Socrates encouraged us to do, we begin to gain more clarity about our place *in* the world and what unique traits and talents we can share *with* the world. Asking questions helps us to determine if we need to let go of certain beliefs or situations that no longer work for us. As we explore who we are, we can go beyond the limits of who we are allowing ourselves to be and expand into our fuller selves. This helps us live in harmony with ourselves and others and ultimately to live with more purpose and meaning. OPA!

OPA! AFFIRMATION

I find joy and meaning in my life when I engage with deeper purpose and know myself.

7

Engage with Arete

The afternoon sun was beginning to fade as we made our way along the winding road to the mountain village of Ano Meros.

"This is the village—we walk in the village," said Elsa with a playful smile on her face as she pulled her car into a small spot at the entrance of the village.

As we began our walk through the narrow lanes, we could hear bells in the distance, a sign the sheep were coming in from their daily adventure in the surrounding hills.

"Tell us more about your parents and growing up in the village," we asked Elsa.

"They didn't need many things," she replied simply. "They just wanted to be good people."

They just wanted to be good people—the phrase resonated within our hearts. Indeed, it wasn't one that we heard often, as we were used to being surrounded by people focused primarily on "having" versus "being," and on "getting" instead of "giving." As we continued our walk, we wondered if we could ever be as virtuous as Elsa and her parents were.

Elsa's words reminded us of the Greek philosopher Epictetus and his suggestion that what matters most is who we are, not what we do for work or how much we have. What matters most is the type of person we are and the type of life *we are living. It was clear to us that Elsa and her parents embraced the ancient Greek value of* arete.

The fundamental challenge for living and working with meaning is to understand how to achieve the good life. Unfortunately, the notion of the good life has been hijacked by advertisers and portrayed as a life in which we seek pleasure, relaxation, and, of course, material goods. This is not the good life that the ancient Greeks advised us to pursue!

The Greek concept of *arete* is one of the key personal attributes or qualities that enables a person to live the good life, that is, to live a successful and *meaningful* life. Arete translates to *virtue* and pertains to the concepts of character and excellence. In simple terms, the notion of arete relates to the deep personal convictions or guiding beliefs we have that form our character, which, in turn, determine how we behave in life. Part of our purpose in life is to learn how to behave!

"Virtue consists more in doing good than in receiving it, and more in doing fine actions than in refraining from disgraceful ones."
—ARISTOTLE

Excellences

A virtuous person is one who has the ability to act well and do the right thing. *Virtues* are the traits, characteristics, or "excellences" as Aristotle called them, that we can measure ourselves against as we strive to be the best we can be. Examples of virtues are courage, honesty, and compassion. The opposite of virtue is *vice*, which is an immoral habit or practice. Obviously, we want to develop virtues, not vices, in order to become the kind of people we aspire to be.

The concept of arete is not limited to benefiting one person but is related to our usefulness in society and how we can use our "virtue and excellence" to benefit *all* of society. Aristotle believed that the greatest virtues are those that are most useful to others. In this context, the commonly heard phrase "living the good life" means that we are acting well and living for society, not just for ourselves. John F. Kennedy crafted a famous line that exemplifies this virtuous thought: "Ask not what your country can do for you—ask what you can do for your country." (Unfortunately, today it appears we have shifted into more of a self-centered "what can my country [or politician or others] do for me" mode of thinking.)

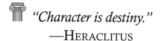 *"Character is destiny."*
—HERACLITUS

The ancient Greek philosophers recommended that we develop our mind, body, and spirit to achieve our best or highest potential. The primary virtues they believed were necessary for doing this, and which appear most often in their works, are the following:

- *Integrity* (including justice, honesty, fairness, truthfulness, respect, righteousness, trust, dependability, duty, personal responsibility, and personal accountability)
- *Love of Learning* (including practical wisdom, continual learning, education, self-improvement, curiosity, open mindedness, creativity, and knowledge)
- *Moderation* (including self-restraint, self-control, temperance, self-discipline, and modesty)

Other virtues mentioned in their writings include the following:

- *Compassion* (including humanity, friendliness, kindness, generosity, forgiveness, empathy, and love)
- *Courage* (including bravery, strength, endurance, patience, perseverance, resilience, and fortitude)
- *Gratitude* (including enthusiasm and optimism)
- *Loyalty* (including valuing friendships, community, honor, unity, and mutual respect)
- *Physical Strength and Beauty*
- *Pride* (including self-esteem, humility, and magnificence)
- *Simplicity*
- *Wittiness*

Some say that wisdom is the most important virtue and some say it is courage, while still others say it is a combination of mutual respect, honesty, and personal accountability. It is important to underscore that, despite being discussed by the Greeks thousands of years ago, all of these virtues are still relevant to living the good life, the *meaningful* life, today!

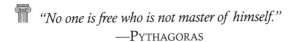 *"No one is free who is not master of himself."*
—PYTHAGORAS

"For a man to conquer himself is the first and noblest of all victories."
—PLATO

The Greek philosophers also advised that if we strive to *do* our best (versus *have* the best), then we will live with excellence. Socrates is credited with challenging Athenians to reflect beyond the rules, laws, and morality imposed by the city-state when deciding how they wished to behave and how they would choose to live their lives. This was a big turning point, as well as an existential milestone, in the history of philosophy.

ENGAGE WITH *ARETE*

*"A person's value does not depend on his qualities but
on the way he uses them."*
—ARISTOTLE

The virtues Socrates and his fellow philosophers discussed
and espoused also went beyond the moral virtues to include
virtues of physical strength and beauty.

*The pursuit of excellence and continual improvement are
fundamental Greek principles that can be found in the spirit
of the Olympic Games. First held in Greece in 776 BC with a
simple foot race, the Games symbolized the pursuit of excellence with athletes competing to show strength of mind, body,
and spirit. The joy of the Games was in the competition, not
in the reward. The winners were crowned with wreaths not
medals. Because many of the athletes were warriors in their
regions but needed to travel in safety to Olympia where the
Games were held, the Olympic Truce was formed to halt all
battles for the duration of the Games. The Games soon became a symbol of peace amongst otherwise competing regions.
The Olympics were held every four years from 776 BC until 394 AD when the Romans banned the Games; they resumed
in 1859. In 1896, the marathon race was established in recognition of the Greek runner who, more than two thousand
years earlier, in 490 BC, had run from the town of Marathon
to Athens to announce that the Persians had been defeated in
the Battle of Marathon. In 1928, the practice of the Olympic
Flame began, which has also helped to keep the spirit of the
original Games alive. The Flame is lit at the beginning of
the Games and then extinguished at the closing ceremonies.
Every four years a new flame is lit at Olympia, Greece, and
then the Olympic Torch is carried from Olympia to the sta-
dium where the new Games will be held. Runners, who have
the good fortune to participate in this time-honored tradition,*

pass the lit Torch from one runner to the next, being careful not to extinguish it. The passing of the Torch symbolizes coming together in international friendship.

The ultimate goal and deeper meaning of the Olympic Games are to unite the world in the pursuit of excellence.

Habit

Some believe arete, or virtue, is spiritual in nature and a gift from the gods and therefore can't be taught. Others believe that arete is a trait that can be learned and therefore can be taught.

"Excellence is not an act but a habit."
—ARISTOTLE

Aristotle believed that, at first, virtue must be enforced by discipline but, over time, it becomes a pattern of behavior and a habit that is second nature to us. We believe that everyone has an inborn capacity for excellence and that virtue can be taught and cultivated, achieved through reflection about ourselves and the goodness of others. Every action we take contributes, for better or worse, to building our character, and with every action we become the person we are. For example, if to respect others is a virtue we hold dear and we show respect for others each day, it soon becomes a habit, an ingrained part of who we are. Alternatively, if we choose to disrespect or lie to others, these actions will, in turn, become habit and part of who we are. Habit grows out of thinking and doing the same thing over and over again until it automatically controls and directs our activity.

"We are what we repeatedly do."
—ARISTOTLE

Our character and personality are formed through our habits, these repeated modes of thinking and action. Everything we do shapes us, molds us. Everything we do contributes to the person we are and will become. Manifesting our life destiny all depends on what we choose to pay attention to and what we ignore, what our priorities are and what they are not. To be a virtuous person, each of us is challenged by life—our life—to develop the right habits and the right character every day. By the same token, being excellent means that we put in the extra effort to go beyond the ordinary and seek to be *extra*ordinary. Rather than electing to simply slide by in life and consequently let life slide by us, we challenge ourselves to go beyond the *call of duty* and recognize that life is always calling out to us to excel and achieve our highest potential. We can express our values and demonstrate our character to ourselves and others through our work. We can show up early, for example, learn new skills, and try a little harder.

> *"The more you practice virtue the easier to practice it becomes."*
> —EURIPIDES

All action is preceded by choice. Everything is a choice even if we don't think we are overtly choosing. To choose is a choice and to not choose, to do nothing, is also a choice. We are ultimately responsible for all of our choices.

Choice →Actions →Habit →Character →Destiny

We all have the power and freedom to choose—to choose to do good or bad or nothing. Even our attitude in any given set of circumstances is a choice and is therefore determined by how we decide to use our power and freedom. Importantly, how we use this power and freedom defines our character. Our choices and, ultimately, our character, override whatever circumstances we find ourselves in and whomever we think has control or influence over our lives. In the larger scheme of things, our fate is not governed by others; it is governed in the character that we build *each day*. In this regard, the life and legacy of Dr. Viktor Frankl, who was a Philhellene and our inspirational mentor, meaningfully illustrates that we can become a product of our choices and decisions, not our conditions. (Dr. Frankl was a survivor of the Nazi concentration camps and author of the classic best seller *Man's Search for Meaning*.)

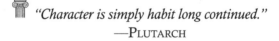 *"Character is simply habit long continued."*
—PLUTARCH

We are who we are because of the many thousands of choices and decisions we have made in the past—and we will be who we will be in the future because of the choices we make today. That is why it is important to focus not only on the *now* but also to envision and plan for the future, so that we may shape our lives and take personal responsibility for steering its course rather than simply floating or drifting through life. As the Greeks say, "He who falls asleep is eaten by the wolf," which means he who is not alert to how he is living, is vulnerable. As we shared in chapter two, the omega (ΩΠΑ) side of the OPA! Coin (awareness) signifies the need to develop the habit of staying awake and looking for dangers and opportunities both now and in the future.

"Man blames nature for his fate, yet his fate is mostly an echo of his character, passions, mistakes, and weaknesses."
—DEMOCRITUS

Our inner world, to a large degree, controls our outer world. Our mental attitude becomes our personality and the lens through which we view the world, which, in turn, influences how we live. To improve our conditions we must first improve ourselves. If we think negative thoughts over and over again, they become a habit and affect not only ourselves but those around us. We might not even be aware that we are focusing on what's wrong with our lives and our world rather than what's right with them. We might not notice that we are focusing on lack instead of abundance, on sickness instead of health, on sadness instead of joy, on pleasure instead of meaning. We might be associating with people who also focus on the negative. In many ways, we become the people with whom we associate. In traditional Greek village culture, there is a proverb, "Tell me who your friend is, and I'll tell you who you are," that refers explicitly to the determining influence of our associations. Having negative people in our lives, more often than not, leads to having negative experiences in life. Hence, it is vitally important to carefully choose our environment and the people with whom we associate because they influence, and often shape, our thoughts and the direction of our life path.

 *"Bad company corrupts good character."*
—Menander

In order to engage and live with arete and purpose, we need to surround ourselves as often as possible with people who talk about the good things that life has to offer, as well as with those who focus on the positive and meaningful attributes of human existence, including prosperity, abundance, health, and well-being. We need to break the habit of thinking weak or negative thoughts and strive to consistently work on having a positive mindset instead. We need to focus on what we want to attract into our lives, not what we don't want to attract. By doing so, we will attract others who believe the same as we do and increase the likelihood of connecting meaningfully with them. Interestingly, the popular, modern-day Law of Attraction actually has roots in ancient Greece, with Plato postulating the first law of affinity, "likes tend toward likes."

Both success and failure are a result of our habits and what we attract into our lives. We can change our habits, of course, if we are aware of our thinking patterns and authentically committed to changing our thoughts and actions. Failure, which is always an option, is largely due to a lack of ambition to correct our poor habits and to strive for excellence.

Love of Learning

According to Heraclitus, "Dogs bark at what they do not understand." We interpret this proverb to mean that people tend to react negatively to things they don't understand, perhaps by barking at them or arguing or even by doing the opposite, dismissing them as unimportant or insignificant. For example, some people bark at the economy: They complain that bad things happen to them; that everyone in politics is corrupt; that everyone in business is greedy (and not interested in offering good products and jobs to support the community); and that the rich control all the levers of the economy, so it's not even worth trying to participate in such an unfair system.

Aristotle said in his classic work *Metaphysics* that "all men by nature desire to know." Is this true? Do all people desire to know about the world and how it works? Do all people desire to know about the paradoxes of life and the incoherencies in the economy? Do all people desire to understand things and put them into context? Or was Aristotle just an optimist and a dreamer?

*"We are lovers of the beautiful, yet simple in our
tastes, and we cultivate the mind."*
—THUCYDIDES

*"The pleasures of the mind are greater than those
of the body."*
—EPICURUS

To Greeks, the love of learning, or *philomathia*, is rooted in the strong belief that they are related to very wise ancestors who had invented or advanced such things as architecture, democracy, literature, mathematics, medicine, music, philosophy, science, and theater, and that it is their individual and collective responsibility to build on what their ancient relatives have handed down to them. By demonstrating their love of learning and setting high expectations for themselves as a result, the Greeks are able to both honor their proud heritage and continue making meaningful contributions to their (and our) *way* and *quality* of life.

*"The foundation of every state is the education of
its youth."*
—DIOGENES

Based on ideas from Plato's Academy and Aristotle's Lyceum, the Greeks believed that the goal of education was to develop wise and meaningfully engaged citizens. Even today, they believe that education should address all facets of the human being: *intellectual* (math, geography, history, astronomy, and science), *cultural* (the history of society, politics, philosophy, music, poetry, and literature), *physical* (gymnastics and sports), etc. If a student learns all areas of knowledge, he or she can become a well-rounded citizen, remain engaged in societal affairs, and contribute meaningfully to the state and society as a whole. In other words, the

Greeks believe passionately that education serves not only the individual but the wider community. If education fails, then the entire village fails.

The spirit of the student must first be conditioned by good learning habits, just as land must be cultivated to nurture and advance the healthy growth of new seeds. There is no sense pushing knowledge on a student if the student does not understand and fully appreciate the *meaning* behind the pursuit of knowledge. No amount of additional funding or number of teachers will produce a wise citizen if the student does not understand this meaning and, as a result, have the desire, authentic commitment, and self-discipline to learn. In the final analysis, it is the student's *responsibility* to choose to learn. It is the student's responsibility to develop the self-discipline to work hard and set goals. It is the student's responsibility to understand that the pursuit of knowledge should be chosen over the pursuit of short-term pleasures or other distractions. If a student chooses not to learn, the student will have to live with the consequences of this choice, just as anyone would, for the rest of his or her life.

"Not by ignorance but by deep learning can people judge properly."
—PLATO

Education aimed at cultivating the love of learning is not about students sitting in a classroom and absorbing information, nor is it about teachers just layering new material over new material on students. Education that is firmly grounded in the Greek concept of philomathia begins within the student—in his or her mind and desire to learn. As Socrates taught, education is about learning *how* to think, not what to think. Echoing this connection, many Greek elders we met on our odyssey wisely told us, "The key difference in life is how you choose to use your mind."

"If a man neglects education, he walks lame to the end of his life."
—PLATO

"Education is the best provision for the journey to old age."
—ARISTOTLE

Greeks value the love of learning as a way to express arete or excellence. They put the mind and its cultivation ahead of materialism. They believe that their intense desire to know and understand the world around them, and their desire to learn and improve themselves and their world, is what opens doors to new and expanded opportunities. They know when all is said and done, education is about *character* as well as about credentials; and, importantly, they also know that it's about the integration of mind, body, *and* spirit.

Integrity

On our odyssey, we decided to spend one evening in the port town of Rafina before having to depart early the next morning from the Athens airport. The best way to reach Rafina was by taxi so we hailed a local cab to take us to our destination. Intuition told us that Panos, our taxi driver, was special—perhaps it was his spirit or how passionately he leapt out of his car to load our suitcases into his vehicle.

"Do you want to hear Greek music?" he asked with pride as we started on our way.

"But of course!" we answered and sat back and enjoyed the views of the countryside while Greek music filled the air.

Upon reaching our hotel in Rafina, we asked him how much the fare was. "It's thirty-six euros but don't pay me now. You can pay me tomorrow morning when I pick you up again to take you to the airport. I will pick you up early—at 4:45 AM. If you are not here," he joked, "I will come up to your room and wake you up with cold water!"

Sure enough, there was Panos at 4:30 AM the next morning, waiting outside our hotel, beaming from ear to ear, and still wearing the same clothes he wore the day before. We thanked him for his exemplary service; getting a taxi anywhere so early in the morning is not the easiest task. We also remarked how trusting he was that he didn't require payment from us the day before, which is something that might not have happened in other places.

Panos looked at us with surprise, then smiled, and simply said, "It's my job."

Do what you say you will do. Keep your word to yourself and to others. Walk your talk. This is integrity. It's a commitment to live in alignment with our core beliefs and with who we are. Integrity also relates to the state of being complete or undivided. When we live with integrity, we are not divided or separated from our core essence—we are whole. The same is true for organizations: Working with integrity means that an organizational entity knows what it is and that all its actions are united or aligned with its core beliefs.

We would never make a product that we would not give to our children.
FAMILY MOTTO OF THE FOUNDERS OF FAGE,
GREECE'S LEADING YOGURT COMPANY

In tough times, we need to understand and trust others, especially those in the corporate and public-sector worlds.

We need to know what is real and authentic. We need to know who is behind the curtain—who are the people operating today's organizations. As with any relationship, we yearn for *humanity*; we want to know who others are and what they stand for, and trust that they will communicate and act with integrity. When we all choose to live and work with integrity, we can build more meaningful relationships, or connections, with one another and build a world that works for all. Integrity, in this sense, serves as a major determinant for engaging with arete and, as a result, with deeper purpose.

> *"Only perform such acts that you will not regret later."*
> —PYTHAGORAS

One opposite of virtue is evil. Being evil or doing evil is a choice. However, the ancient Greeks believed that everyone was essentially good and that no one in his or her right mind would choose to be evil, to do wrong. They believed that a person who does wrong must be doing so out of ignorance for he or she did not know a better option existed. Why, for instance, would anyone ruin another's property, private or public, by defacing it with graffiti? Why would anyone steal money from a vulnerable old person? Why would anyone add a little extra to an accounting bill or manipulate others into doing more or paying more than their fair share? Putting mental illness aside, they must be doing so because they are ignorant. They must be doing so because they don't understand the bigger picture of how we are all *interconnected*: What one person does affects another and, in the end, affects everyone. They didn't realize that they were setting an example, a very poor one at that, for others to do wrong as well.

"To do injustice is the greatest of all evils."
—PLATO

A person's true character is often revealed when no one is watching. Some may ask, "Why not? If no one is watching and there isn't really any penalty for doing wrong, why not do whatever I want?" They rationalize that the bad thing they are doing is actually a good thing because it benefits them, their family, or their situation. They believe, in other words, that the end justifies the means irrespective of what others may think or feel. The end (expressing my art) justifies the means (defacing someone else's property with graffiti). The end (gaining money) justifies the means (stealing from the elderly or padding an accounting bill). The end (gaining power) justifies the means (manipulating others or cheating the system). They're not thinking of the impact their actions have on others or what their actions say about them. They're not thinking that the village may break down if everyone did what they did. They're not caring about others; with these actions, they're showing that they care only about their own personal gain.

But the end and the means are the same thing when it comes to the subject of integrity and character. We are who we are when no one is watching. We are who we are especially under adversity—our character will be exposed when we are under pressure or face difficult times. We cannot say or do one thing in public and then do the opposite when no one is watching.

"I'm looking for an honest man."
—DIOGENES, as he walked through the streets of Athens with his lantern, in broad daylight, searching for a virtuous person, one of good character

126

In regard to the financial crisis in Greece, several villagers shared their views about the lack of respect and personal responsibility surrounding the theft of public funds that had occurred, by simply stating, "The fat men ate all the money." They believed strongly that if *arete* existed, they wouldn't need laws and rules to tell everyone how to live—everyone would just know what was right. When the existence of arete is low, or doesn't exist at all, then laws are needed because people aren't taking personal responsibility to live right and respect others in the broadly defined *village*. Against the backdrop of the Greek crisis, the twin issues of integrity and responsibility could not have been more important, especially for those entrusted with managing the public's business and guarding the public trust. The Athenian playwright Aeschylus, who is often credited with inventing the tragedy, cautioned, "It is not the oath that makes us believe the man, but the man the oath."

The Greek tragedy style of drama began in Athens in the fifth century BC with the works of Aeschylus, Euripides, and Sophocles, and played an important role in helping people see and learn from the suffering of others. The plays explained how people failed, and in doing so, evoked feelings of fear, pity, and sympathy from the audience. As we see from these tragedies, sooner or later our wrong deeds will catch up to us and we will suffer the consequences. Sooner or later, any attempt to profit from the weakness of others will eventually lead to our own suffering.

The ancient Greek word "akrasia" means weakness of will and the lack of self-discipline or control over one's self. Socrates, like many of the other Greek philosophers, was a true optimist because he believed that if people had the right information, they would exercise more control over themselves. However, we often act against our best interests. Even if we know that a certain action is better than another, frequently we choose the worse action. For example, we know that eating an apple is healthier for our bodies, but sometimes we choose to eat sweets instead. Socrates would argue that we chose the sweets because we thought that they were better (perhaps rationalizing that they were better tasting and more pleasurable, thus making them the better choice). Socrates would also argue that we made this choice in error; due to our ignorance of what was really the better choice (the apple). This line of thinking leads us to have more compassion and understanding for those who make poor choices or even for those who do evil—in many cases, they are simply ignorant and unaware that there are better choices and that they could have chosen more wisely.

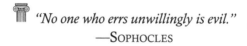 *"No one who errs unwillingly is evil."*
—SOPHOCLES

Speaking the Truth

*One day, a young shepherd boy, bored and lonely, devised a way to have some company. The shepherd cried "Wolf!" and the villagers ran to his pasture to help him, only to discover there wasn't a wolf. A few days later, the boy tried the same trick and again, the villagers came to help him, only to discover there wasn't a wolf. The next day, a wolf actually came to attack his sheep and the shepherd cried "Wolf!" but this time, the villagers just ignored his cry for help. **Speak with integrity if you want to be believed.***

—*Aesop's Fables* (Greece, ca 620–560 BC)

To honor others and the village we must cultivate relationships that are based on truth and integrity. We cannot say one thing and do the opposite. Eventually, if we don't walk the talk, it will catch up to us. As one villager warned us, "Everything that is true will be revealed. The olive oil and the truth always rise to the top."

🏛 *"The greatest virtue is to say and act the truth."*
—HERACLITUS

To live with arete and integrity means we endeavor to be who we appear to be. To live with arete means there is a connection between what we believe and what we actually do. There is a connection between what we say we will do and what we actually do. Our words and actions advertise who we really are.

🏚 *From the child and from the fool, one learns the truth.*
TRADITIONAL VILLAGE WISDOM

If we choose not to live with integrity, our hearts and spirits will know and we will stop believing in ourselves. If we don't believe in what we are saying or doing, sooner or later, others will stop believing in us as well. This applies not only to our personal, everyday life but also to our choice of work. It is important that we choose work that reflects our arete, our virtues—if we don't, we are effectively living a double life where our work is one thing and our real self is another.

When we live with integrity and truth, we are being true to ourselves. Pythagoras advised us to "always choose the way that seems best, however rough it may be." When we resist the temptation to take the easy route, we become stronger.

Summary

The Greeks strongly believe in the concept of living up to one's full potential and living a life of arete by developing and integrating the mind, body, and spirit. Throughout the ages, they espoused that if one builds virtue and character first, success and prosperity will follow. This stands in stark contrast to some other philosophies that espouse that one needs only to believe in something and it will be brought into existence. Again, while the law of attraction can be traced to the ancient Greeks, they have always firmly believed that success results from hard work and that it flows *through* you, not to you, as a result of your emotions *and* actions. In this sense, we build arete one day at a time.

Socrates reminded us that it is not living per se that really matters, but *living rightly*. It's all about our choices. Arete is about knowing what is right and *doing* it. As we become more aware, we can start to stand up for what we believe in, set higher standards, make better choices, and live a life full of good acts based on our chosen virtues. With time and life experience, we become the kind of person we want to be. Staying true to who we are gives us energy and a strong foundation for finding more joy and deep meaning in our lives. In times of crisis, arete keeps us on our *meaning*-focused path so that we aren't easily swayed by others or by the events around us. By regularly practicing and building arete, in other words, we also build our capacity to *respond* to life's challenges more effectively and engage life with deeper purpose and meaning.

OPA! AFFIRMATION

I find joy and meaning in my life when I engage with deeper purpose and arete.

8

Engage with *Evdemonia*

*"**Everywhere you look, there is** something magnificent looking back at you. That's why I love Greece," remarked a traveler seated beside us at the local taverna in Santorini, which overlooks the Aegean Sea. "The beauty is endless— just look at that sunset—amazing. Haven't seen a sunset like this for years," he continued. The way he spoke made us feel like he was just waking from a deep sleep. "Been too busy working to take time to travel, but now, now that I've 'made it,' well, now I have the time and money to see what I've been missing all along," he added with a smile.*

"Do you really feel like you've been missing something?" we asked, curious to hear his insights.

"Yes. I spent so much time working but really, to be honest, at the end of it all, I have to admit it wasn't that satisfying. I'm not sure why I put so much effort into it, other than, of course, to make money and buy things. But now, I definitely want to do something more meaningful with my life—after all, there's only so many days left," he reflected, catching his breath before he continued. "That's why I came to Greece—to walk in the footsteps of the ancients and get some inspiration for my life. You know, I see how they live here. They don't need all the things we have; gosh, I have more clothes in my suitcase than some of these villagers

have in their whole closet, and the interesting thing is, they seem to be so much happier. They seem to be in touch with who they are and with life . . . much more than I am or my friends back home are."

We could tell already that this was one of those conversations where all we had to do was ask one question to get a whole story back in return. The traveler seemed to be on a meaning quest and needed to talk, to share his thoughts.

"Yes, Greece is a small country with a big heart," he continued. "They sure seem to know what's important here . . ."

As the sun began to set, we knew that it was going to be a very interesting conversation and a very interesting evening.

Prosperity

It seems that some of us don't really know what we want in life. We pursue wealth, power, and things. We've been conditioned to believe that these are symbols of success—the more the better. "After all, whoever has the most toys wins." Having money and things has become the end goal because we can count it, keep score, and use it to compare ourselves to others. But when we don't look the way we should, or if we don't have the same amount of wealth or abundance of things as others do, we trap ourselves into thinking it is we who are not enough. Such feelings of inadequacy typically lead to stress and depression.

Money, of course, is needed to pay for our necessities. However, the challenge that most of us face is that we keep redefining what our necessities are. We get one thing and determine that we also "need" the next. We reach a certain level of wealth and materialism and then worry that it isn't enough. Happiness and living the good life, we think, is always just one thing away. Once again, much like the Greek hero Sisyphus (who was ordered to push a boulder uphill for eternity), our quest for happiness and living the good life becomes an endless—and joyless—undertaking.

"Nothing is enough for the man to whom enough is too little."
—EPICURUS

Unlike the Greeks in the traditional village who don't see very much, if any, advertising, we are bombarded and overwhelmed with advertising messages each day that seek to create new needs and wants. Unlike many of the Greeks we met in the villages who wear the same clothes all week, we want different outfits to wear every day. Unlike many of the Greeks we met in the villages who are satisfied with a donkey, or a car or a scooter that works, we want shiny new cars with all of the latest features. And unlike the Greeks in the village who believe they have enough and only take what they need, leaving the rest for others, we are focused on wanting, getting, and taking all we can get.

We justify it by saying that this is the "American dream"—work hard, earn lots of money, buy lots of things. Soon we start to identify ourselves with our money and material things. *I am what I have* becomes our subconscious mantra for living even if we are also unaware of what we're really doing and what impact it has on our lives. This situation creates envy—we want something so badly that we may go into debt to get it, we may manipulate others to get it, or we may even steal it. The elusive end, in other words, justifies the means—with the end defined in terms of financial and material wealth and the means referring to anything that can be done to reach it. We all know people who can't seem to control this urge for more and who can provide ample justifications for their obsessive-compulsive behaviors, even if they can't or won't see them as such. They want everything they see in a store or at a buffet or at their neighbor's house. It becomes a quest with a life of its own, a deep-seated insatiable need. And ultimately, they may lose their souls in the pursuit of more money and more *stuff.*

> *"Men's ambition and their desire to make money are among the most frequent causes of deliberate acts of injustice."*
> —ARISTOTLE

Greed, of course, comes in many forms. However, greed, in its most fundamental sense, stems from *fear*—the fear of not having enough, of not being successful enough, or of not being seen as valuable enough. Greed also comes from a perception that we live in a world of scarcity, not abundance, and that survival requires competition over cooperation and collaboration. The recent financial crisis in Greece and around the world has brought to light many of the issues with our excessive consumerism, out-of-control debt, and yes, boundless greed. Left unchecked, excessive wealth and power tempt and corrupt our character. As Panos our taxi driver in Athens so wisely said, "Many Greeks are destroying the way it used to be. Now they are using money to make decisions instead of our traditional Greek values."

The Greek god Dionysus granted King Midas one wish. After some thought, Midas proclaimed, "I wish that everything I touch would turn into gold." His wish was granted. Everything Midas touched did turn into gold and he became a very wealthy man. However, Midas soon discovered that his wish had unintended consequences. He could no longer taste his food since it would turn into gold, and he could no longer

enjoy the company of others since they, too, had turned into
gold. This famous Greek myth highlights the consequences of
excessive greed—"Be careful what you wish for."

The question is, "How much is enough?" We hear all too often, "When I reach my number, when I have a million dollars, I will feel secure, I will be free, I will be happy." Others focus on hoarding things, believing that they will be, or at least feel, more secure if they get and keep just one more thing in their always-growing supply of material stuff. Still others fill their lives with an overabundance of food, sex, and other addictions, believing they will feel more secure and happier if they just have "one" more of whatever it is they feel they *need*.

> *One day, a dog carrying a bone in his mouth crossed a small bridge. Looking down into the water, he saw another dog who appeared to be carrying an even larger bone than his. But when he opened his mouth to bark at this other dog, he inadvertently dropped his own bone into the water. The dog didn't realize that the other dog was actually his own reflection and that the bone he saw in the water was actually his own bone. His loss—he didn't appreciate what he already had. **The desire for gaining more, for gaining something bigger and better, can be an illusion.***
>
> —Adapted from *Aesop's Fables*

The costs, whether intended or unintended, obvious or hidden, of the hunt for more are staggering. We postpone true happiness while we are busy seeking and trying to get more. We ignore our relationships while we focus on accumulating more. We overlook our health in our chase for more. Getting more is actually making us sick from all the stress of worry and overwork. And the sad thing is, we are spending our valuable time making money to buy things we might not even need!

"*Riches do not exhilarate us so much with their possession as they torment us with their loss.*"
—Epicurus

Wealth can be lost like the bubbles in a bottle of champagne. Money and things can be taken from us at any time and often for any reason. Unfortunately, some people spend so much time and energy accumulating wealth, only to spend even more time and energy trying to protect what they've accumulated for fear they may lose it, along with, sadly, their individual "identity."

Our money habits reflect how we view and relate to the world. If we hoard money or material things, we may be feeling insecure about our long-term future; feeling like a frantic squirrel worried about whether it has put away enough acorns to make it through the winter. Again, rather than abundance, we may see scarcity in the world, worried that there isn't enough to go around. Alternatively, we may spend money recklessly, wanting to show others how much we have or to trying to fill a void of meaning in our lives. Either way, how we save or spend money is a magnifier of how we feel about ourselves, how we relate to the world around us, and what we find to be meaningful in our lives.

An old man owned a large piece of gold. Afraid it would be stolen, he decided to bury it in his flower garden. Every day, he would dig up the gold, look at it glitter in the sunlight, and then replace it once again in the hole he had dug. One day a robber, after watching the old man worship his gold, decided to take it. The next day, the old man arrived in his garden to find his gold

> missing, and in its place, an empty hole. He cried out in anguish and his neighbor came to find out what was wrong. "My gold, which I admire each day, is missing," sobbed the old man. "Just put a stone in the hole," advised the neighbor. "After all, what use was your gold—you weren't doing anything with it anyway." **Wealth unused might as well not exist.**
>
> —Adapted from *Aesop's Fables*

The ancient Greek philosophers put money and wealth into perspective for us. They believed what is important is not the total amount but how it is used. They believed that money must circulate. It must flow to and from us or, in a truer sense, it must flow *through* us. What we receive, we must also give to the world. If we use money for the good of others, we are opening the door for more good to flow through us.

> "If a man is proud of his wealth, he should not be
> praised until it is known how he employs it."
> —SOCRATES

Money, in this context, is more than a vehicle simply for the exchange of goods and services; it can be viewed as a form of spiritual energy. As such, money is good if it is used in service, broadly defined, and if it keeps circulating. Cut off the circulation flow, however, money can quickly morph into the root of all evil.

> "Try to make money a thing to use as well as to
> possess. It is a thing to use to those who understand how
> to enjoy it and a mere possession of those who are able
> only to acquire it. Prize the substance you have for two
> reasons—that you may have the means to meet a heavy

*loss and that you may go to the aid of a worthy friend
who is in distress. For your life in general, cherish your
possessions not in excess but in moderation."*
—Isocrates

The Greeks we met on our journey seemed to enjoy life more and shared more of what they had with others. They appreciated things more because things were harder to get in the villages and on the islands. Their houses may have been small yet this caused them to gather in the village *plateia* (square) or local *kafenio* (café) to socialize. Their local church may not have had any bells, yet they would find a way to summon people there by banging on pots and pans. While we might complain about what we *don't* have, the Greeks we met simply worked with what they *did* have. They truly believed—and still do—that they have enough.

*"He is a wise man who does not grieve for the things
which he has not, but rejoices for those which he has."*
—Epictetus

"Yes, we have the crisis now but we've had worst in the past," the villagers told us. "From a bad winter will come a good summer." Onc observable benefit of the financial crisis is that the villagers know deeply in their hearts that their identities, sense of hope, optimism, and authentic happiness aren't tied to *external* things. "We have few wants," explained YiaYia Toula. "We aren't so covered up with things. We know what's really important in life."

"By desiring little, a poor man makes himself rich."
—Democritus

Hippocrates, a Greek philosopher and the father of modern medicine, warned us, "Everything in excess is opposed to nature." Pythagoras offered a tempered view on this issue with the following: "Do not spend in excess like one who is careless of what is good, nor be miserly; the mean is best in every case." Antisthenes, a philosopher who was a disciple of Socrates, advised us to reduce the things we possess to the bare necessities in order for our souls to be free. Each of these great thinkers would agree that we must be mindful that although we can possess money and things, we should *not* be possessed by them.

During a drive down the mountain after visiting several small villages in Western Crete, we reflected upon the difference between needs and wants. We asked each other: "What if we went back to living in a small hut on the beach or in a Greek village—what would we put in the hut? What would we really need versus what would we want?" We began with our list of necessities and then moved onto the second category: things that might be seen as unnecessary but were things we wanted. We soon realized there was a third category: things that were highly unnecessary. Unlike the Spartans, who lived simply, didn't own much, and believed everything should have a purpose, we seemed to have a long list of things that we thought were both necessary and wanted. "But where in the hut would we put all these things we think we need and want, especially all the clothes, books, and kitchen accessories?" we asked each other. Our awareness grew. We realized that it wasn't a question of being materialistic or being totally antimaterialistic. It was really about being more aware of the role money and things play in our lives. We concluded that the ultimate goal is to first find inner prosperity and meaning in our lives and then layer on any materialism, as opposed to starting the other way round—embracing materialism and then hoping one day to find meaning.

For the Greeks we know, accumulating lots of money is not their ultimate end goal in life. They don't want to spend all their time and energy on making money. They have other priorities. Our cousin Iakovos told us, "If you focus on money you will be unhappy, but if you focus on life, living life, you will be happy. I have my health, my family, my friends, so therefore I am happy." On another occasion, he told us, "Time is not money. I want to spend my time with people I like and people I love. That is the secret to a meaningful life."

Beyond Happiness

"Life, liberty, and the pursuit of happiness" is a well-known phrase from the introduction to the U.S. Declaration of Independence. Thomas Jefferson and the founding fathers built upon the advice of the ancient Greek philosophers who taught us that *happiness* was the end goal, the highest good or purpose that we should attempt to achieve in life. However, the ancient Greeks were actually referring to a much deeper and meaningful concept called "evdemonia," which over time has been incorrectly translated into the idea of happiness that we know and use today.

The root words in evdemonia (ευδαιμονία) are "ev" (ευ), which translates to well or good, and "demon" (δαίμων), which refers literally to divine possession or what we refer to as spirit. Evdemonia, in its true form, is a complex *metaphysical* concept and therefore transcends or goes beyond customary definitions of happiness that are grounded only on a physical or emotional plane. Evdemonia is both holistic and integrative in its meaning, seeking to combine the elements of body, mind, and spirit into a much higher, more enlightened state of human existence. Against this multidimensional backdrop, evdemonia relates to a deep sense of well-being, inner prosperity, fulfillment, and the best possible condition of being alive. All our life experiences, both in good and challenging times, contribute to our personal sense of evdemonia, whereas only our pleasurable or good experiences contribute to our state of what is commonly referred to as "happiness."

We often view happiness as a positive emotion, one that is highly desired and closely related to pleasure. Happiness and pleasure are essential to life, but the challenge with both notions is that they are short-term feelings that come and go depending on our circumstances. Happiness is often associated with pleasurable experiences, which, as we all know, can vary widely and disappear quickly. For instance, some of us find happiness in shopping, dining with friends, and partaking in sports activities or a long walk alone in the woods. If we pursue happiness, often we are delighted by the highs of pleasure but are disappointed when these feelings subside, creating a rollercoaster of emotions within us. We may feel content and happy at certain moments in our lives but these are *feelings* of contentment and happiness, not the deeper evdemonia that the Greeks espoused as an ultimate purpose or end goal in life.

We view these *feelings* of happiness as "hedonistic happiness," which unfortunately tend to motivate many of our decisions both in our everyday lives and at work. Often hedonistic happiness is related to acquiring things; we desire something and are happy when we get it, but soon the novelty wears off and we desire something more and the cycle of desire continues. Hedonistic happiness, in other words, is fleeting and a moving target. It's dictated by things, events, or other people—all *external* to our self. This represents momentary happiness, which can elicit moments of feeling "good," but it is not the kind of *authentic* evdemonia achieved and sustained over the long term.

> "Happiness [evdemonia] demands not only complete
> goodness but a complete life."
> —ARISTOTLE

Evdemonia, in short, is closely associated with living well, living the "good life," or as we call it, "the *meaningful* life." As our very wise relative Diogenes shared with us, "Evdemonia means the complete life. We in Greece know about this concept but I'm not sure the rest of the world knows about it!"

> "Happiness [evdemonia] is an activity of the soul in
> accordance with perfect virtue."
> —ARISTOTLE

Some people try to define or refer to evdemonia with words like "flourishing," but such descriptors are still too limited a translation of this *meaning*-focused concept. In many ways, animals can flourish; however, evdemonia is unique to humans because it involves deep reflection, faith (in a spiritual not necessarily religious sense), reasoning, and good actions. Aristotle, like Socrates and Plato before him,

MEANING

FLOURISHING

HAPPINESS

believed that evdemonia could be achieved through the proper development of our highest potential as human beings, which involves knowing ourselves, developing arete (excellences, virtue, and character), and taking "right" action.

Fulfillment

True fulfillment is measured not at the surface of our being but deep within our soul. A truly fulfilled person knows that she or he is in the right place, connecting with the right people, doing the right type of activities or work. These individuals know that they are answering the call from life or are conscious of the deep-seated feeling that there is something more they are supposed to do with their life. They know that they are always in the transformative process of developing their full potential, gaining in wisdom and experience, expressing who they truly are as individuals, and importantly, creating the life they really want to live. In short, they realize that life is a journey, an odyssey, and that it is an ongoing search for meaning, which is their primary, *intrinsic* motivation for living.

If our purpose in life is to strive to become our best self, then our dear friend Lucia Rikaki is a great example. Following her passion for filmmaking, Lucia and her team founded the Hippocrates International Health Film Festival, a unique event that focuses on viewing, discussing, and appreciating films from around the world on the topic of good health. The festival, which was initiated on the island of Kos, Greece, the birthplace of Hippocrates, was appropriately named in his honor.

In May 2011, ironically, abruptly, and sadly, Lucia discovered she had inoperable brain cancer at the age of forty-nine. While undergoing intensive medical treatments, Lucia chose to find meaning in her situation and even found the energy and will to create a film with music using her x-ray MRI images to share the story of her journey with others. Her purpose filled her with joy and lifted not only her own spirits but the spirits of those around her. Despite heroic efforts from the medical staff in Athens, Lucia succumbed to her condition in December 2011.

Lucia did not measure the success of her life by the amount of money or power she possessed; but rather by how she connected meaningfully with her core essence and found her place in the universe doing what she most loved. She will always be remembered as a person who created joy and meaning in her life, who sought to do the same for others, and who truly lived The OPA! Way.

Everyone's journey to obtain fulfillment and meaning in life is unique. No two people can take the same path, nor should they. A key challenge many of us face is that we don't know where to start, so we stay stuck, frozen in our tracks. Although we are busy with our daily tasks, we may feel that we are drifting through life, unsure of what we are really supposed to be doing. We sense that we are in the wrong place, or the wrong relationship, or the wrong job. We sense that we are living someone else's expectations for our life, not our own. Our life lacks deep joy and purpose and, by implication, meaning. This lack of fulfillment and meaning in our lives is draining. The Greeks have a word for it, "acedia," which means "absence of caring," "dry spirit," or "lethargy of the spirit."

The antidote for acedia is to find purpose in our lives by striving to know ourselves better. This means going beyond the physical into the *metaphysical* world as we explore who we are and awaken to our authentic selves. This is an opportune time to identify those things we consider to be meaning-

less in our lives so that we may consider what can be done about them. Remaining prisoners of our thoughts cannot be an option if we are really serious about combating acedia!

Inspiration, like enthusiasm, is a manifestation of the *spirit* within us. When we connect with our hearts and ignite the flame within us, when we express our spirit, we become more *true* to ourselves, more authentic. And when we answer life's call, we start to shift the perception of who we are, who we are destined to become, and what we are capable of doing to make a positive, meaningful contribution to the world in which we live.

As we gain knowledge about how we want to define success and become clearer about our purpose, we can start to effectively design our life. Our priorities also become clearer. Putting acedia behind us, we now have more energy and passion to handle the challenges in life, as well as focus on what we really want . . . versus what we don't want.

> *"Let him who would move the world, first move himself."*
> —SOCRATES

Finding fulfillment is especially challenging during periods of transition. We may be facing changes at home due to a move, divorce, death of a loved one, or simply due to our children growing up and walking out the door, leaving our nest empty. We may be facing a change in our job or career, retirement, or unemployment, when we are leaving a community of work behind and struggling with our identity and where we belong. We may be facing a plateau, having felt successful in the past, but now feeling that our current life doesn't really reflect who we have evolved into today. Or our situation may be more extreme: We may be facing a countrywide crisis, like the people have been experiencing in Greece, where everything around us seems to be on the eve of destruction and we feel like powerless pawns in a larger chess game.

Heraclitus gave us insight into the transience of life when he espoused that nothing ever stays still; all is in flux. Change is the driving force behind the transitions in life we experience. It is our personal responsibility, nobody else's, to find new meaning in our lives through each transition.

Whether we like it or not, with each life transition comes a change in identity that must be addressed as part of our search for meaning. We need to ask ourselves: "Who am I now?" In our book, *Prisoners of Our Thoughts*, there is a statement that, in our view, cuts to the chase of this existential challenge: "You can change without growing but you can't grow without changing." In other words, change in our lives is inevitable; however, growth—we're talking about positive, healthy, meaningful growth—is not. Unless we are authentically committed to engaging with our deeper purpose and therefore prepared to "know ourselves" by asking questions, life transitions will seem like nothing more than a merry-go-round rather than an opportunity for true growth, fulfillment, and enlightenment to occur.

Fulfillment in life involves the *complete* life, that is, it involves both our personal and work lives. In this connection, we all know people who may have great careers but are unhappy with their personal lives, and we all know people who are presumably happy in their personal lives but are unfulfilled in their work lives. We should not view work as being separate from ourselves since it influences so much (our relationships, finances, places of residency and living arrangements, energy levels, etc.), consumes such a large part of our time (we spend about half of our lives doing some kind of work), and is a significant causal factor behind whether or not we feel that we are living a *meaning-*

ful life. Fulfillment, in large part, stems from being able to do the type of work that is consistent with who we are (that is, in alignment with one's core essence, values, and temperament) and that enables us to use and leverage our capabilities to meet our highest potential. If we can find work in which we have a genuine interest and with which we naturally resonate, eventually our purpose in life will become clearer. But what is really most important is *who* we are and who we want to become, *not* what specific job we choose to do or career path we choose to pursue. Pursuing our life purpose is about making a life, not simply making a living.

The fulfilled life, in other words, is a journey in pursuit of excellence and evdemonia. Life is a natural, transformational process of getting to know ourselves over and over again—a continuous process of self-discovery, renewal, and fulfilling our potential until we take our last breath. The Greek philosophers believed the good life, that is, the *meaningful* life, in the final analysis, is measured most accurately and reliably on our deathbed: We will feel fulfilled if we do not harbor serious regrets or misgivings about our unrealized, *unfulfilled potential*. At the same time, we will experience evdemonia if we have a deep sense of satisfaction, knowing and feeling that we have done the best we could to answer our life's call to meaning.

Philanthropy

"The greatest virtues are those most useful to other persons."
—ARISTOTLE

A key part of evdemonia is to extend beyond one's self in service to others. The ancient Greeks believed that our talents were given to us to share. By helping others improve and transform their lives, by helping others find meaning, we ourselves will improve and find meaning in our own lives.

The word "philanthropy" is rooted in the Greek words "philo" (love) and "anthropos," which refers here to mankind or "humanity." Philanthropy, in other words, literally means "love of humanity." Unfortunately, today, the deeper meaning of the word philanthropy has been lost in translation. It has become misunderstood to mean "an act or financial gift made as a charitable donation." If we embrace the original, larger, and more accurate definition of the word, it expands our understanding to include all actions that show we care about and want to improve the quality of life for all humanity.

From a philanthropic perspective, a major challenge facing much of our thinking in the so-called postmodern world is that we mistakenly believe that the primary goal in life is *self*-actualization—focusing on becoming the best we can be, only for ourselves (and then perhaps for our families). We complain that we have to deal with enough stress just caring about our own lives and the lives of our children. We say, and by implication try to justify, that we can't *give* any more to others. This restrictive mindset, once again, stems from thoughts of scarcity and fear, not abundance and courage.

If we fail to give, who then will care about and be responsible for the village? Plato believed that we can only find our true selves in service to others. The happiness, well-being, and evdemonia of the village are just as important as our own *individual* happiness, well-being, and evdemonia. We must complete the circle, becoming the best *we* can be while helping the *village* to become the best it can be.

We see some people struggle with the concept of giving to others because they fear that if they give something, they will lose something. Some fail to give because they are so busy competing and trying to get ahead of everyone else. Others give but do so reluctantly, out of guilt. Still others give only to show off, to build their image as a good person, or to get a tax write-off. All these motivations indicate a belief in scarcity, the lack of *inner* prosperity, and the inability to give freely, openly, and authentically.

We need to gain deeper insight into both the *intrinsic* meaning as well as the *extrinsic* meaning behind why (and how) we give or don't give. We need to ask ourselves if we are manifesting the true meaning of philanthropy as originally espoused by the Greeks, and doing our fair share to take care of the village.

> *"Where your talents and the needs of the world cross, there lies your calling."*
> —ARISTOTLE

Some of the elders with whom we spoke on our journey shared with us that their only regret in life was that they didn't try to help others more. We should learn from their experience and wisdom. We all have a role to play in making our village *and* the world a better place. There is so much that needs to be done. There are so many people in our villages and in our world who need help. In our own small ways, we can love humanity by helping others with education, with food, with health, with clean water, with the environment . . . or simply by helping others feel that they belong. There are so many ways we can add deep and meaningful value to the lives of others and, in doing so, add deep value and meaning to our own lives. All we have to do is look for, and be open to, opportunities to serve and to make a positive, meaningful difference in the life of the next person we encounter on our personal odyssey—a "pay it forward" way of living. The end goal of this kind of authentic philanthropy is evdemonia not only for ourselves but for others. Then before we die, we can feel fulfilled knowing that, by extending beyond ourselves, we were committed to meaningful values and goals and did our part to leave our village (our world) a better place!

Philanthropy at Work

Just as people can extend beyond themselves to demonstrate that they love humanity, so too can organizations. However, today, in Greece and around the world, organizations, both corporate and governmental, are facing a significant lack of public confidence and trust, which, in our view, really stems from the broader and more deeply embedded Crisis of Meaning. Traditionally, organizations, especially in the private or corporate sector, have been focused on the numbers—maximizing profits by minimizing costs, and with it, maximizing investor or shareholder value. (Although public-sector organizations, by definition, are not profit driven, they do operate on similar principles and are under increasing pressure to behave more businesslike and maximize the public's return on investment.) The problem with this mechanistic approach is that there is too much focus on the *financial* return to investors and not enough focus on the *meaning* of the organization, which affects all stakeholders, including employees, customers, constituencies, partners, and the broader "village." When the only stated goal of an organization is to *make* money (or account strictly for the expenditure of money, as is the case for government and nonprofit organizations), people tend to follow the money, *not* the deeper meaning and purpose of the organization. For example, hospitals may no longer focus primarily on the larger meaning of healing, health, and well-being; likewise, food companies may no longer focus primarily on the larger meaning of providing nutritious food that supports and advances health and well-being.

While nonprofit organizations are viewed generally as being good and caring toward humanity, for-profit organizations are viewed by some as just the opposite: evil and greedy. In some circles, "capitalism" is a dirty word, one that provokes hostility and anger. Indeed, the notion of *free-market* capitalism can easily become an emotionally charged issue and lead to different forms of political action, from peaceful protests to more aggressive behaviors, even lawlessness, coupled with calls for large-scale systems change. In the name of fairness and of reducing the economic divide between the haves and have-nots, proposals to do away with capitalism, or at least institute major reforms in the current free enterprise system, are commonplace. Without a doubt, for-profit organizations, most notably those corporations that were deemed "too big to fail" or that are guilty by association for society's social and economic inequities, are now more vulnerable than ever to this kind of volatile public sentiment. In light of the recent financial crisis in Greece and in other countries, such vulnerability among for-profit organizations has become especially evident. Against this backdrop, the demand for *virtue* is rising at a very fast pace, and organizations need to respond to this demand—if for no other reason than for their own survival.

With the growing interconnectedness of the world and increased transparency resulting from the internet, organizations in all sectors are slowly responding to this call for change. We believe that it's time to adopt a broader, more humanistic approach to work and business. It's time to shift from the antiquated, singular focus on *profit* to a new, broader focus on *meaning*. We call this "meaningful capitalism," or with a unique Greek twist, "anthrocapitalism" (combining *anthropos* [humanity] and the English word "capitalism").

Our meaning-focused perspective on capitalism is not about corporate social responsibility per se, which is often a separate initiative that is layered onto the organization. It's not about making a profit and then setting aside some of it to give to charity. It's not about bringing business practices to the nonprofit world. Rather, it's about a whole new model that starts from and stays connected to the Core of Meaning. It's about *how* an organization makes its money. It's about clarifying and developing a common understanding of the deeper *meaning* of the organization: why it exists, the broader difference it wants to make in the world, and the broader social significance of its products, services, and programs. It's about rethinking how the organization connects with and supports the well-being of *all* stakeholders. It's about shared value and purpose. It's an *outside-in* approach—looking at the broader and deeper meaning of what the organization is doing for society—versus the traditional, inside-out financial approach, such as how much money is needed by the organization to "make" this quarter? Anthrocapitalism is a new, *meaning*-focused way to look at capitalism from a humanistic perspective, that is, focusing the organization on doing good while still meeting its obligation to maximize long-term investor value.

People's relationship to work is changing. Increasingly, people want to find more meaning in their work. They want more opportunities for personal growth, to make a meaningful difference, and to contribute to a cause larger than themselves. Meaning should be the cornerstone of the culture of any organization, across all sectors (private, corporate, public, government, nonprofit, etc.) and industries. As the primary intrinsic motivation of human beings, meaning represents a source of energy that, if harnessed and leveraged with integrity and respect for the human spirit, drives everything to its intended, highest goal. The primary role of leadership, then, is to lead *with* and *to* meaning by designing and sharing a clear "meaning message," or powerful story about how the organization brings meaning into people's lives. A well-crafted meaning message can help change how employees view their work, how customers view the organization's products and services, and how the local community and society-at-large view the organization's contributions. People want to work for, buy from, and be associated with organizations that find meaning by improving lives and making a positive difference in the world.

Like people, when an organization is authentic, knows itself, and operates from its Core of Meaning, others will respond positively to it. High levels of trust, engagement, innovative thinking, productivity, and loyalty all come from the Core of Meaning. Conversely, if levels of trust, engagement, innovation, and productivity are low, we have found that lack of meaning is often the primary cause.

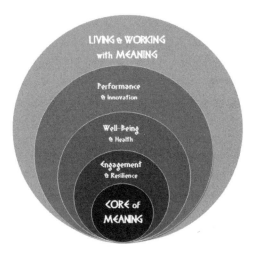

Like people, no two organizations are the same. Each must discover and then operate from its own core essence, which gives it unique meaning and a unique role in the world. Each must view its work in the larger context of seeing what needs to be done in the world, seeking to serve the greater good, and committing authentically to make a meaningful difference in the lives of the people it serves and in the environment within which it exists. Like the challenge facing people, the organizational challenge is not about a trade-off: make money *or* advance meaning through improving lives. Both people and organizations can do *both*, and they should, for this is their *destiny*. And by fulfilling their destiny, in the end, both people and organizations leave their *legacy*—their "soulprints" of meaning—on the world.

Meaning is the new bottom line. It is integral to the business model of the new millennium. The shift toward meaning signals a new role for organizations, especially for those in the corporate sector. The influence of this meaning-focused paradigm shift should not be underestimated. It holds the potential to rediscover the very "soul" of capitalism and, by extension, bring forward a *moral transformation* of the way that business as usual is conducted in all types of organizations. If businesspeople thought of themselves as *anthro*capitalists, helping and caring for humanity, rather than simply as capitalists fixated on profits, the image of business would improve dramatically in the eyes of the public.

Summary

Many of the Greeks we met along our journey seemed to face life sure of who they are and where they belong. Perhaps they weren't so covered up with material stuff like so many of us are, so it was easier for them to just be themselves. Perhaps they were more grounded in their history and culture, so they knew their roots and how they were connected to the world. Perhaps they just knew how to simply live from their Core of Meaning.

In our world of fast-paced change, increasing complexity, and "predictable" uncertainty, it is now even more important that we build our lives focused on purpose and meaning rather than on pleasure, power, and money. Although some may say that meaning comes from happiness and success, we strongly believe that it's the other way round—happiness and success, in the final analysis, come from meaning. Meaning is the foundation and primal source of energy in our lives. When we know and are conscious of the underlying principles of our lives and work, we can operate from this deeper sense of understanding and meaning. We can live with *inner* prosperity and put the other aspects of living (material things, money, and other forms or symbols of *outer* prosperity) into a more meaningful context. When we know better *who* we are, we will discover *what* we need to do in the world, and then we can move with confidence toward realizing our full potential and truly engage with deeper purpose and evdemonia. What matters most at the end of our life is that we feel that we have made the best of ourselves and have given back more than we have taken. With so much suffering in the world, with so much need, the ways to contribute and make the world a better place are infinite.

Every person has the capacity to find joy and meaning in his or her life and work. By knowing thyself, by living and working virtuously with arete, and by seeking fulfillment through evdemonia, we can become more of ourselves and engage with deeper purpose. In doing so, we discover that we matter, that we are part of something special, and that our lives do, indeed, have meaning. OPA!

OPA! AFFIRMATION

I find joy and meaning in my life when I engage with deeper purpose and evdemonia.

Part Four

ATTITUDE (A):
Embrace Life with Attitude

9

Embrace *The Fullness*
of Life

Greece, like life, is a *feast to be enjoyed. Just as we savor the last drop in a bottle of wine, we savor each moment in Greece, cherishing the sunshine and most of all the people. The Greeks we met were in love with life. They threw themselves into it and bathed in the joy of living.*

Throughout our odyssey, we asked many Greeks, "Why are the Greeks so passionate about life, even during the crisis?" Violetta from the village of Plaka told us, "It's in our blood, it's in our veins, it's in our DNA." Giorgos from the Blue Palace Hotel in Elounda told us, "Every day is unique. Today is an especially nice day—not too sunny, not too hot, not too windy, just right. We are happy because we enjoy each day and because we go out after work and socialize with our friends." Maria told us, "We squeeze life, just like we squeeze all the juice from the lemon!" Panos, our taxi driver in Athens told us, "The secret to Greek passion is that we use our mind to live for today." Mihalis, at the classically beautiful Veneto restaurant and hotel in the heart of old town Rethymno, told us, "No one understands the Greek mentality. You have to feel the Greek mentality."

The Greeks taught us that it isn't just about living, it's about living well. It's about celebrating life, even if another crisis looms around the corner.

Some philosophers believe that joy and meaning in life can be found by detaching ourselves from life and from any challenges that we might face. In doing so, we can relieve ourselves of suffering and enjoy life more. However, the Greeks we encountered on our journey were adopting just the opposite philosophy—they were embracing life, *all* of life, *all* the ups and downs, *all* the joys and the sorrows. They were not detached from life; they were fully attached and immersed in life. While some Greeks were clearly suffering during the crisis while chaos was gripping the country, for the most part, especially in the villages and on the islands, the people we met were embracing and celebrating the fullness of life. "Life is to be lived. Come celebrate life with us," urged our friend Andonis. "Feel life, taste life, love life," he continued waving his arms with great enthusiasm.

Greece is a place to celebrate what it means to be human and to be truly alive. The Greek approach to life is one of nonresistance. The Greek phrase "agape zoes" means "love or zest for life" and signifies being open to and taking in the fullness of life.

Nikos Kazantzakis (1883–1957) is one of the most important Greek writers, poets, and philosophers of the twentieth century. His novels are well known: Zorba the Greek *(which became an Academy Award–winning movie),* The Greek Passion, Captain Michalis, The Saviors of God, The Last Temptation of Christ *(also made into a Hollywood movie), and* Freedom or Death, *among others.*

The epitaph on his grave bears his words: "I hope for nothing. I fear nothing. I am free." Kazantzakis taught us how to appreciate life by living life to the fullest, expressing ourselves, feeling free, and even living a little dangerously. Aristotle had said, "No great genius has ever existed without some touch of madness," and Kazantzakis followed with, "A man needs a little madness, or else he never dares cut the rope and be free."

Through his writings, Kazantzakis shows us that we need to embrace the "full catastrophe" of life, that there is beauty in all the chaos of life, and that "life is trouble, only death is not." In Zorba the Greek, *the most famous scene occurs at the very end when the wooden structure that Zorba and Basil had built as part of an innovative business venture collapses. Zorba laughs off the defeat, saying they will just start again and rebuild. Basil, who up until the time of this catastrophic incident had demonstrated extremely uptight and risk-averse behaviors, then turns to Zorba and surprisingly asks, "Teach me to dance." They spread their arms out, snap their fingers, and begin to dance the sirtaki, a popular Greek dance, on the beach. Basil was really asking Zorba to teach him how to live, how to laugh at life, and how to really feel fully alive, no matter what life brings.*

To know death is to know life. The ancient Greeks taught us to reflect on death in order to live better today. Life is fragile. In a moment, our light could flicker out and we could be gone. Tomorrow may never come. When we realize that we have limited time left, and that we are always moving toward death, we can start to live each day to the fullest. We realize that life is precious and that we should not waste whatever moments we have left. As we traveled throughout Greece we saw many widows wearing black, the symbol of death and mourning, which would put our day and lives into perspective. Each day is a gift and, like Zorba, we all should devote time to dance on this earth because one day, inevitably, we will be under it!

We both know that we don't want to reach the end of our lives, only to realize that we didn't really live them to the fullest. We don't want to look back on our lives and realize that we worried about the same thing for ten, twenty, or even thirty years. We don't want to take our lives for granted and, most importantly, we don't want to die with regrets.

Nikos Kazantzakis wisely taught us to "die every day" and "be born again every day." The uncertainty of life teaches us—or at least gives us the opportunity—to reflect upon what we still want to do and say. Our relative Diogenes warned us, "If you want to do something, you should do it now." That's why the Greeks believe there is always time for coffee, there is always time to connect with one another and enjoy *today*. As our cousin Alexandros said to us, "We will worry about work tomorrow but not now—now we eat and drink. We will deal with tomorrow, tomorrow."

> *"What a strange machine man is! You fill him with bread, wine, fish, and radishes, and out comes sighs, laughter, and dreams."*
> —NIKOS KAZANTZAKIS

The Greeks taught us to loosen the reins and, in a sense, surrender to life so that we may fully experience more of it. Every day is a new day to be enjoyed, not simply endured. Every day is a chance to appreciate even the smallest of life's pleasures, as Homer reminds us: "Dear to us ever is the banquet, and the harp, and the dance, and changes in raiment [clothing], and the warm bath, and love, and sleep." We mustn't wait for life to begin by saying, "Once I get a new job or a new relationship, then I will be happy and fulfilled." As we've noted before, life doesn't just happen *to* us; we happen to life and we make it meaningful. As the sun sets on yet another day, we need to ask ourselves, "Did we squander the opportunity to truly live today or did we grab onto life for all that it's worth?"

Unlocking the Greek Key

The notion of living to the fullest by grabbing on to life and holding it tight can be traced to ancient Greece. Our research into how Greeks embrace the fullness of life can be viewed as a meaningful display of how life becomes art and how art, in turn, can become life. Take, for example, the decorative Greek design known as the "Greek key." Typically we see this ornamental pattern, which consists of repeated, continuous vertical and horizontal lines (often in relief), used artistically as a decorative border on buildings, clothing, pottery, and other artifacts.

Sample "Greek Key" Design

The Greek key has deep roots in ancient Greece. This decorative element was referred to as a meander, or meandros, in ancient times and had a profound meaning. The word "meander" came to refer to the twisting and turning path of the Maeander River (also spelled Meander), which is in what is now southwestern Turkey. Since then, meander has also been used to describe a winding pattern or design. Over time, it has taken on new meanings and usages, suggesting that *to meander* is analogous to moving aimlessly and idly without any fixed direction or purpose. Hence, we now hear uninspiring phrases, such as "meandering through life," to describe a form of aimless wandering judged to be devoid of authentic meaning.

For some twenty-five hundred years, the true origin, interpretation, and use of the Greek key, or meandros, have remained locked away. We'd like to acknowledge two individuals in Greece whose groundbreaking research into the true meaning and significance of the Greek meandros cannot be overstated. Michael Kalopoulos is a prolific and best-selling author and scholar in the history of religion. Kalopoulos found that the meandros was not intended to simply be a decorative symbol for use in art. On the contrary, the historical and mythological origins of the meandros revealed that it was a special hand grip used in ancient Greek gymnastics, especially in the sport of wrestling; in the "pankration," a Greek martial art that was a popular event in the earliest Olympic Games; and in battle.

According to Kalopoulos, on a physical plane, the meandros grip was the unique coupling of the hands that was a powerful way to hold combatants securely. On a much higher, metaphysical level, the meandros grip was a manifestation of the heroic and resilient Greek spirit. Metaphorically speaking, it enabled ancient Greeks to challenge the gods. The *symbol* of the meandros was a reminder that human beings held in their hands, literally and figuratively, the capacity to face with confidence whatever happened to come their way in life. Against the most formidable of odds, both internal and external, the meandros reminded them that they and no one else held the secret to their ultimate destiny. Relying on the meandros grip also meant that they had a *purpose* in life and were not "meandering," through life or wandering aimlessly, as the term is commonly (mis) understood to mean.

The Meandros Grip[2]

The second source of enlightenment regarding the Greek key came from what at first seemed an unlikely source. A popular Greek singer, Giannis Miliokas, took a leave of absence from music to study the origins of the meandros. In 2010, he published a book, *Meandros: The Unknown Gymnastics of the Ancient Greeks*. In it, Miliokas describes, in similar fashion to Kalopoulos, the meandros grip both as a technique for subduing and securing opponents of different kinds and as a symbol of the capacity of human beings to overcome adversity no matter how great the odds. (Both authors noted that even Plato, who was an avid wrestler, was aware of the meandros grip.) Miliokas goes further by suggesting that the meandros grip symbolizes unity and strength *within* one's being, as well as in meaningful connections with others. He also reveals the many health benefits in body, mind, and spirit that result from exercising the meandros grip in *all* areas of life. In this context, the common saying "get a grip" (on life) takes on an entirely different and inspirational meaning!

---

[2] This image is an adaptation of the "meandros grip," created from multiple sources.

Expression

The Greeks invented theater, including the genres of drama, comedy, and tragedy, which reflect the range of emotions and the fullness of life. What's interesting is that theater, especially drama, isn't just for the stage! On a trip to Corfu, we were awakened by the loud voices of a couple engaged in what we thought was a rambunctious argument. When we asked our friend what was going on, she laughed and said, "They are just having a conversation over breakfast. They're not arguing—they're just talking loudly and passionately. They're Greek!"

We've been in many kafenia and tavernas when someone starts a debate, usually about politics, and before you know it, everyone in the place joins in. Usually it starts slowly: someone offers an opinion, after which another person, perceiving that they know more about the subject or that they are the expert, offers a counteropinion, and it goes on from there. The more intense the debate, the louder the participants become. They're typically not hard of hearing. They are just loud, excited, passionate people. (Perhaps it is the loudest person who is perceived as the one who is "right"!)

The Greek spirit involves expressing oneself—in body, mind, and spirit—without reservation. Being *enthusiastic* to the ancient Greeks was a manifestation of expressing the spirit within. The Greek way is to speak loudly and laugh even louder. Greeks speak with their whole bodies, especially with their hands. Their hands fly like flags blowing in the wind. The more they believe in something, the more they use their whole bodies to communicate it. In short, it's about passion and emotion. The conversation rises like a wave at high tide and then, after everyone has expressed his or her opinions, the conversation recedes and all is relatively calm once again. We refer to it also as the Greek "flash," which is usually followed by laughter and the invitation, "Let's eat!"

In contrast, a (non-Greek) person once said to us, when we disagreed about something, "Let's keep the emotions out of this." And we had to wonder, "How do you do that, if you are human? How do you go through life without expressing your true feelings, thoughts, and opinions, or at least without trying to express them? Should we just sweep issues, especially matters that are really important to us, under the rug and pretend that they aren't there, that they don't exist?" Unlike the Greek approach to expressing oneself, this sounds like a sure way to anesthetize or crush the human spirit rather than elevate or unleash it.

> *"Every word is an adamantine shell which encloses a great explosive force. To discover its meaning you must let it burst inside you like a bomb and in this way liberate the soul which it imprisons."*
> —NIKOS KAZANTZAKIS

To express ourselves is good for our spirit and a good way to relieve stress and get the blood flowing. Expressing ourselves shows that we are confident and have deep inner *self*-esteem (as opposed to *other*-esteem). "If I don't express myself, I will burst, I will explode," said our friend Zoe, whose name, interestingly, means "life." "We Greeks are very emotional people. We go up and down. We are loud, especially when watching a sports game—we shout without hesitation when a goal is scored or when a goal is missed. We can't hold back. We have to let our spirits free. We have to feel alive."

Expressing our "self" is an important part of our innate *humanness* and inalienable right as humans. The Greek word "parrhesia" means to speak freely, to say what's on our mind, and to speak the truth even when it feels risky. Being direct helps us to avoid the challenge of having to guess what someone else may be thinking, leading to more transparent and authentic relationships. Expressing ourselves openly and freely also helps to build our enthusiasm, which in turn raises our energy level and inspires not only ourselves but also those around us.

 *"Your silence gives consent."*
—PLATO

Greeks genuinely believe that to remain unexpressed is a shame. They know that holding emotions in and letting them fester blocks the flow of energy in our bodies and eventually leads to sickness. Not expressing ourselves because we are afraid of disapproval, or simply because we lack enthusiasm, produces a flat-line approach to life that is doomed to failure.

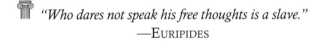 *"Who dares not speak his free thoughts is a slave."*
—EURIPIDES

Strikes and protests are accepted as natural activities in Greece because they represent the freedom to express dissatisfaction against actions that are believed to be oppressive. The strong desire to express oneself is deeply rooted in Greece's long history of wars and foreign occupations when civil liberties were suppressed:

- Aeschylus, an ancient Greek playwright (ca 525–ca 455 BC) is credited with the line, *"It's better to die on your feet than live on your knees."*
- "Freedom or Death" is a famous motto of Greece, tracing back to the War of Independence (1820s), when the Greeks rebelled against Ottoman rule.

- Oxi (pronounced *o-hee* or *o-chee*) Day is celebrated every October 28 to commemorate the day in 1940 when Greek Prime Minister Ioannis Metaxas faced an ultimatum made by the Italian fascist leader Benito Mussolini: Either let the Italian troops enter Greece to occupy strategic locations unopposed, or face war. Metaxas' unequivocal response was transmuted by uttering a simple yet powerful and emphatic "Oxi," the Greek word for "no."

What other country celebrates a "No Day"? The celebration of such a unique event illustrates how much the Greeks value and even encourage rebellion against being told what to do and against anything they think is unfair, including foreign occupations, certain government rules and regulations, excessive taxes, and even some traffic signs!

We had to smile one day while driving our friend Yannis to an appointment. The sign in front of us said "No Entrance" yet Yannis insisted, "Ignore the sign and go through. The sign doesn't make any sense. This is the most direct route to our destination." When, wary of the sign, we protested, Yannis again insisted that it was the best way to proceed. We drove through quickly, relishing in our small rebellion and knowing that we had just become a little more Greek!

Driving in Greece is another form of self-expression. It's definitely an adventure to be embraced with enthusiasm. In Athens, we watch the motorcycles and scooters fill the lanes at any stoplight, jockeying for the front position. When the light turns green, we always feel like we are at the Indy 500 motor race surrounded by the deafening sounds of the engines. One taxi driver also told us that the shortest unit of time in Athens is the amount of time between when the light turns green and the car behind you begins beeping its horn!

In Greece, the rules of the road seem more like proposed guidelines. On many occasions, we questioned whether the double white line along the middle of the road meant some-thing different than we knew, especially in Crete, as cars proceeded to pass one another, whizzing by at breakneck speed. In other countries, the double white line indicates no passing allowed! For all the talk about being a relaxed cul-ture, one only has to travel along the highways of Greece to see that the Greeks do, indeed, have multiple personalities.

It only took us a few trips to the island of Crete to real-ize that the "National Road" was also called the National Highway, E75, the Motorway, the Main Road, the New Main Road, and the New Road! We cherish the simplic-ity of the sign, located just outside of the Municipality of Rethymno, which reads: "New Road ↑ Old Road →." Driving along the National Road is always an adventure. It's not unusual to share the Road with tractors, jeeps, buses, trucks, scooters, motorcycles, bicycles, and the oc-casional donkey. It's not unusual to have to swerve around cars whose occupants have stopped to visit roadside shrines or vendors selling fruit, or simply to pick *horta*. In Greece, people don't "park" their cars, they simply "stop" their cars where and when they need to stop!

Traveling along the back roads, it's not unusual to turn a corner and find that the road has narrowed to a single lane. Sometimes the lane is such a tight fit that we might scrape both sides of our car on the walls of the two houses on either side. We simply pull in our side mirrors and carry on. Sometimes, however, there is no way around a parked or "stopped" car, representing yet another opportunity to meet the locals. Driving on the back roads is yet another metaphor for life—"You never know what is waiting for you just around the next corner."

The Greeks need outlets to express themselves, whether it's through debating politics, driving, or dancing. Greeks dance when they are happy and they dance when they are sad. They dance to celebrate life and they dance to forget about their problems for a while. Traditionally, they also danced to prepare for battle. Each region of Greece has its own folk songs and traditional dances, which are forms of cultural expression that are designed to reach in and touch one's soul. When dancing to the music of the bouzouki or lyre (three- or four-stringed instruments), it's easy to get swept up in the repetitive nature of the rhythms. The very act of dancing and moving one's body is a form of self-expression, which also forces a change in attitude. It's hard to be depressed when you are holding your head high and putting one foot in front of the other in resonance with the tempo of the music and its underlying message.

Living life fully means we are always finding new ways to express our creativity. When we have joy in our hearts and passion in our souls, we are alive with creative energy. When we are inspired, when we breathe energy into our souls, we are open to new connections and have new thoughts and ideas. It's not *what* we do in life, but *how* we do it. When we do things with enthusiasm and creativity, we are able to more fully express who we are and find new sources of meaning. The Greeks taught us to push the boundaries of our lives as a way to meaningfully express and realize our ultimate freedom as human beings. They taught us to be open to taking the back roads in life so we can expose ourselves to many different experiences rather than close the windows of opportunity that life offers us. By staying on the all-too-familiar highway, or on roads that others have chosen *for* us, we rush through life without checking out the scenery along the way. Curiosity and creativity are fundamental to expressing who we are and to living a full life.

Laugh until you have nothing left. The Greeks we met were able to laugh with life. They seemed to be able to take anything that happened and add some humor to it. When the Prime Minister of Greece, Antonis Samaras, underwent eye surgery to repair a damaged retina, the Greeks joked that he needed the surgery because his eyes popped out after seeing the latest financial report on the Greek deficit! The Greeks use humor and laughter to rise above and overcome the obstacles of life, as well as not to take themselves too seriously. Laughter serves to calm the nerves, helps to put life into perspective, and provides a vehicle for escaping the prison of our thoughts so that we don't allow our circumstances to control us and effectively determine our future.

A sense of humor, including the willingness to laugh *at ourselves*, can be a powerful tool, when used appropriately, to cope with all kinds of stressful situations, especially those that are outside of our control. Although we may not be totally free from the conditions or situations that confront us at work and at home, we still can *choose* how we will respond. Humor, in this context, is a practical and meaningful way to exercise the ultimate human freedom to choose one's attitude, no matter what the circumstances.

Choosing our attitude is an important part of expressing ourselves. Our friend Andreas believes that everyone has to learn how to enjoy themselves and also be a little crazy to get through the challenges of life. Our cousin Iakovos told us, "We are all happy on Crete . . . except for the tourists when they first get here. They arrive so stressed and unhappy, and they can't relax. But us, we are happy!" (Coincidentally, we recall meeting a tourist on a bus who told us, "I know I'm on vacation and I should relax but I can't. I don't know how.")

Many people are leading very busy lives but are not fulfilled. They are moving so fast, running from event to event, from activity to activity, focused on what's next. Sadly, in doing so, they are missing out on life. They are "too busy" to stop, look at their lives, and reflect on what's working or not working. Many feel burned out, exhausted, and over-whelmed. They have lost their hope, their spark, and their zest for life. They are simply existing versus truly living.

The slower lifestyle in Greece allows more time for deep reflection, more time to celebrate and appreciate life, and more time to focus on the art of living. This slower pace also has the corresponding effect of resonating with the natural biorhythms (from the Greek words "bios" [life] and "rhythmos" [any regular recurring motion, rhythm]).

Opposites

Greece is a land of stark contrasts: the rustic charm of rural life versus the modern amenities found at luxury spa hotels and the new airport in Athens; the relaxed pace of life on the islands versus the hustle of city life where only fifteen seconds is allowed to cross the street; the patient nature of the Greek people versus their impulsive nature on display, for example, when driving; their desire for precision, per-haps originating from having invented some of the most ad-vanced mathematical principles, versus their desire to adopt many approximate measures in day-to-day life; and so on.

Heraclitus espoused that the world is the unity of di-verse and conflicting opposites. In order to live a full life, we need to recognize that life is full of opposites: life and death; young and old; joy and sorrow; wealth and poverty; beginner and expert; summer and winter; expansion and contraction; light and darkness; good and evil; visible and invisible . . .

Opposites are beneficial because they help us to define and contrast things; we need to know one thing in order to know the other. When we experience sickness, we know and appreciate health; when we experience hunger, we appreciate fullness; when we experience insomnia, we appreciate sleep;

when we experience failure, we appreciate success; when we experience loneliness, we value and appreciate friendship; when we experience depression, we appreciate joy; when we experience limitations, we appreciate freedom; when we experience unemployment, we appreciate employment; and when we experience a crisis, we appreciate calm.

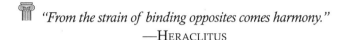

"From the strain of binding opposites comes harmony."
—HERACLITUS

As Heraclitus pointed out, opposites are also needed to achieve harmony and wholeness. At weddings in Crete, for example, the bride and groom offer a small gift of honey and almonds to their guests, representing both the sweetness and bitterness that come with marriage. We need to appreciate *all* events in our lives and take the good with the not-so-good.

Life is about embracing both the joys and challenges of life, not simply going through the motions. It is the wholeness of life that we should be pursuing and embracing, not wishing for balance where the ups and the downs are in equal amounts. A heart monitor shows the ups and downs, the wavelike rhythm of life. If the heart monitor shows a "balance," then the line is flat and we are no longer alive. In this sense, there really is no such thing as balance in life; it is an illusion, a lofty goal that can never be attained no matter how hard we try and how much power we put behind our best of intentions.

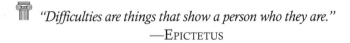

"Difficulties are things that show a person who they are."
—EPICTETUS

Importantly, life is not just about the so-called happy times. Times of struggle and unhappiness are very much

part of the ebbs and flows of life, and it is during these times
that we have the opportunity for deep self-reflection and improvement. More likely than not, these are the times when
we can access the deeper meaning in our lives. Ironically, it
is when we feel "out of sync" that we experience our most
soulful times. And it is during these moments of heightened
awareness that the window of opportunity opens and in-
vites us to reach deep into ourselves, connect with our core
essence, and discover the real meaning of our existence.

To be sure, there is no easy route to happiness—we have
to deal with the challenges that life brings. Through times of
suffering, especially those that are inescapable, we can ask
ourselves, "What do I want and what do I *not* want?" Every
difficulty we experience in life presents us with the opportunity to go inward, to strengthen, and to increase our faith in
our ability to get through tough times. Life always has meaning, even in the most difficult of circumstances. However,
it is ultimately our personal responsibility to discover this
meaning for ourselves. Once again, life doesn't just happen
to us; we happen to life, and we make it meaningful.

"It is not good for all your wishes to be fulfilled."
—HERACLITUS

Unfortunately, many of us don't seem to want to live a
full life—we want to experience only the happy and pleasurable side of life. If we have pain, we want quick relief:
we turn to food or drugs or to someone whom we hope will
rescue us. When considering the bigger picture, some de-
privation is good, some longing is good, some struggles are
good, because they tend to force us to change and, ideally,
to grow. Without these voids and these struggles, without
these tensions between opposites, we might never change.
All of us can recall times in our past when we took steps to

creatively fill the voids in our life as well as when we took steps, perhaps even drastic leaps, to deal with our struggles. Whether we like it or not or care to admit it or not, each of these life-affirming steps has helped to make us who we are today.

Optimism

In the wise words of Heraclitus, "The sun is new each day." We have heard and continue to hear this sentiment echoed throughout Greece. The dawn of a new day brings a new beginning, a new experience, a new day of hope and possibilities. Our host at the Blue Palace in Elounda told us that he looked forward to every day because he strongly believed that "each day is unique" and that each day gives him opportunities to embrace and celebrate the beauty and joy of life.

Wake up each morning and say *kalimera*, which means "good morning" or "good day" to life! The Greeks we met truly believe that life is good; today is good and tomorrow will be even better. Each day, from the traditional Greek perspective, represents a new opportunity to take a fresh attitude toward a particular person, project, situation, or just life in general.

To maintain a positive, resilient, and can-do *attitude* about whatever situation you are facing, we recommend that you take three steps—or make three choices—which, when taken together, form the basis of true optimism. First, you have to believe that you *can* realize your goal(s) *and* adopt a positive, can-do attitude that supports this belief. For example, we *can* exercise and get fit, we *can* have better relationships, we *can* finish school, or we *can* get a better job. In other words, we first have to believe that our goals *are possible*. To be sure, things may be difficult, but, in our true optimist way of thinking, they are not impossible. Second, we must be able to visualize in our mind's eye the possibilities that will lead us toward our goal and what our lives will look like when we get there. Third, we must be able to manifest the spirit within, that is, feel the passion and enthusiasm that will help us actualize possibilities and reach our goals. In short, truly optimistic people believe in themselves and what they are capable of achieving, they are authentically committed to maintaining a positive and resilient attitude about achieving their aim, they *see* the possibilities of what can be, and they are passionate and enthusiastic about taking the action(s) needed to make the possible a reality.

Despite the economic crisis, the Greeks we met were very optimistic, proud, and notably resilient people. Having overcome so much in their history from foreign occupations, famines, wars, political unrest, and so forth, they know how to survive and believe that they will come out of whatever societal challenges they must confront stronger and wiser. "Now we suffer but something good will come from it" and "The storm will pass. We will get through this" are representative of the optimistic comments we heard frequently throughout our journey.

We always have the freedom to choose our attitude. Our thoughts determine if what we choose to believe is possible. When we hear a negative comment, we always retain the right, and therefore always have the ultimate freedom, to turn negativity into possibility.

When we change our attitude, our circumstances change, not necessarily the other way round (waiting for our circumstances to change to then change our attitude). In the final analysis, our capacity for discovering meaning is determined by our state of mind and how we perceive a given situation.

Gratitude

The Greeks have a saying "ola einai kala," which means "all is well." This saying was shortened to "ola kala," meaning "all well," and then shortened again to the now familiar "OK." Despite the crisis, many Greeks with whom we spoke still genuinely believed that life was OK. Giorgos, a waiter at Cul de Sac kafenio, told us, "I am happy. I have my wife and children, I have my job, I have my village where I can go, I have my health, I am strong. I don't need much." Our relative, Diogenes, shared the following insight with us, "Greek people know what is important. For instance, if you could have only one thing because of the financial crisis, which would you choose: a cat, a dog, or a fishing boat? Yes, the fishing boat because you can catch fish to eat—it is a necessity and something for which we are more grateful." Many other Greeks told us, "I have my health so I am good." They understand and are grateful for the basics in life.

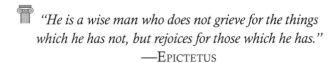

"He is a wise man who does not grieve for the things which he has not, but rejoices for those which he has."
—Epictetus

Instead of focusing on what we don't have in our lives—what is missing—it is best to be grateful for what we *do* have. Indeed, it's all about perspective. We can appreciate that life is actually easier today than it was in the days of the ancient Greeks. Today we have many conveniences and amenities that we shouldn't take for granted, such as electricity, automobiles, indoor plumbing, medicines for just about anything that ails us, telephones, automatic dishwashers, public transportation, bicycles, computers, etc. And, of course, we should also try to appreciate the vast beauty that is all around us every day. By being *grateful* for and honoring what we have received and what we've experienced in life, we will open ourselves to discovering more and deeper meaning in our lives.

> *"If all misfortunes were laid in one common heap whence everyone must take an equal portion, most people would be contented to take their own and depart."*
> —SOCRATES

To be sure, things could always be worse. Others may be suffering more than we are. If our house has declined in value, someone else may not even have a place to live. If our feet hurt, someone else may have lost a foot. If we lose an eye, someone else might have lost both eyes and be permanently without sight. Be grateful.

Our friend Mathew told us, "Most Greeks don't need much. But many of us, especially in the cities, are changing. We have become like others who have lost their understanding of the simplicity of life. We are trapped by money and materialism. We become like animals, wanting more, tearing at a pile of money, gorging. It is crushing our spirits. We feel trapped in the system. We are giving up our uniqueness in order to participate in the world economy. We are losing our core values and we are forgetting to be grateful for what we have in Greece."

Many of us go through life on autopilot, oblivious to the good and inherent richness to be found all around us. We need to practice having a grateful attitude by acknowledging and demonstrating an appreciation for at least one thing per day. Even if we don't enjoy everything about our lives or work, we can still express gratitude for the parts that we do enjoy or at least find meaningful. Again, it's all about attitude and perception. We must give attention to what is good or going well in our lives and what has the potential to be even better in the future.

"Rejoice over the good things which come to you, but grieve in moderation over the evils which befall you."
—ISOCRATES

Just as the mythological Atlas was condemned to hold up the earth on his shoulders, many of us appear to experience life hunched over, heavy with and punished by its burdens. Most people, at least those with whom we would ideally like to associate, won't want to be around us if we always act like a victim of our circumstances, complain incessantly, and seem ungrateful for all that is good in our life. Other people, because they are like-minded and kindred spirits in a more healthy and positive way, will join and connect meaningfully with us *if* we enjoy life and are grateful for what we have. The law of attraction, like a life magnet, works both ways!

Against this magnetic backdrop, there are two views of the world: one of scarcity and one of abundance. We see what we want to see. Perception does not always mirror reality; oftentimes, however, it becomes *our* "reality." When we believe that there isn't enough of this or that in our lives, or when we focus on the fear of losing something, we are effectively living our lives in a world of scarcity. When we focus on doors closing in life, we will see more closed doors and, more often than not, miss the doors that are unlocked or already open.

Conversely, if we believe the world is abundant with pathways to unlimited opportunities, we will expect to see as well as attract, good things flowing to us in life. In this very different and promising scenario, our hearts are open and we believe that there is truly enough to go around. We also believe that there are really no lost opportunities because, if one door closes, another door will open.

There will always be more fish in the sea, but the fish will not automatically come to us, we have to go out and get them, as well as feel grateful when we catch them. Opportunities are ever-expanding but we must learn how to create and discover them for ourselves. This is our personal responsibility, although it need not be viewed as a burden to be carried, like the world on Atlas' shoulders; rather, it represents a part of our personal odyssey in life and a natural manifestation of the human condition. Hence, we can learn how to become healthier, have better relationships, be financially secure, engage in meaningful work, enjoy life, and help others, if (and only if) we hold ourselves responsible for both *learning* and *doing* them. We can, in other words, transform our lives by modifying or shifting our beliefs about our abilities as well as the opportunities that are facing us. By doing so, we can live larger and more meaningful lives and spread our gratitude and generous view of the world to others.

Time

Much has been written and said about "Greek time," referring to the fact that Greeks seem to operate with a different sense of time than others. Even though they invented some of the most advanced concepts in mathematics, the Greeks like to be, shall we say, flexible, when referring to time. Three or four hours might mean four, five, or more hours, depending on the circumstances. When we asked the guard when the museum would be opening after the renovations were completed, he joked, "Who knows. It could be two years, it could be two thousand years. Only the gods know!"

For the Greeks, time unfolds as it should. There is a natural process for everything in life. There are natural cycles, seasons, and reasons for things. One must be patient. For example, some people do their best work while in their twenties while others use their life experiences to do their best work in their sixties and beyond. Life brings everything in good time; there is a perfect and natural moment for everything.

The Greeks take a longer view of time. Many other countries focus on the short term and instant gratification but the Greeks focus on the long term, realizing that things will work out, eventually, *over time*. The gods and the ancient philosophers lived thousands of years ago, so ten or twenty years feels like nothing in Greek time! No need to hurry because everything will still be here. No need to chase time. No need to stress out over the day-to-day challenges of life. As our friend Giorgos told us, "No need to check your email. The world won't stop just because you didn't check your email. And if the world did stop, what better place to be than in Greece!"

The Greeks take time to savor their food, engage in conversations with others, and enjoy the moment while dining versus rushing through the experience asking, "Where's my food? Where's my bill?" The Greeks know that life is to be lived to the fullest, not rushed through, and they also know that waiting another fifteen minutes after dinner to relax in the company of others is good for our digestion and our overall health.

Some of the ancient Greek philosophers, namely the Stoics, believed that life is transitory so we should live in the present moment. Heraclitus also believed that life was transitory and ever-changing, but he espoused that we couldn't really live in the present moment because, technically speaking, there is no *present* moment—that moment has just happened and is now in the past! Therefore, we recommend that we focus on enjoying the flow of life in its entirety, rather than get caught up in what is commonly referred to as "the now."

We can't live in the past since the past, like a broken plate, has already happened and there is nothing we can really do about changing it. What is in the past is preserved in that past. We can also enjoy the present and connect with what is right in front of us, in the flow of the moment. But, again, if we focus only on the ever-present, we will be ill-prepared for the future. If we quit school at too early an age or if, like the farmer, we fail to plant anything, our future may be bleak. We must have a vision, a purposive goal or aim of something to pursue; something that will inspire, motivate, and pull us into the future. As the primary authors of our own life movie scripts, we must commit to visualizing and anticipating the possibilities that can lead us to a better tomorrow and more positive future. Not doing so, in all likelihood, will only result in our becoming stuck, and perhaps even sick or depressed. We must focus on both the *present* and the *possibilities* when answering life's call.

Life is made up of many moments. It is a continuous path that is forever changing. To be sure, it is important for us to enjoy and appreciate the moment for what it's worth along the time continuum. At the same time, it is also important for us to clarify and, hopefully, understand where our path, our personal odyssey, is headed and where along that path we happen to be at any given point in time.

Summary

We are all looking to feel more fully alive, to feel freer, and to feel more human. Whether we are facing a crisis in our lives or watching others face a crisis, we all can benefit from reflecting on what's really important and embracing the fullness of our lives. The true meaning of the Greek key, or meandros, reminds us to grab on to life and live it to the fullest. It's about being fully aware of how we are living our lives—why we think what we think and why we do what we do.

Expressing ourselves—being in touch with and honoring *all* of our emotions—shows that we are embracing *all* of life, not simply tiptoeing through it. Being open to the opposites in life—the ups and downs, joys and sorrows—helps us to understand what we really want and what we don't want. Focusing only on the upswings of happiness is unrealistic, misguided, and regrettably causes us to miss the richness and fullness of life.

Life doesn't just happen to us; we are responsible for creating the lives we want. We must strive to be optimistic and focus on the things we can do, so we keep moving forward, versus focusing on the things we can't do and getting stuck. As our friend Nikos said, "You only live once, but if you live right, once is enough!" If the Greeks taught us anything, it is to embrace *all* of life—the universe is abundant and generous to those who do!

OPA! AFFIRMATION

I find joy and meaning in my life when I embrace the fullness of life.

10

Embrace *Aphobia*

***The surname Pattakos (Παττακός) is** derived from two
Greek words: patasso (Πατάσσω; meaning to "crush" or
"punish") and kako (κακό; meaning "evil," "harm," or
"wrong"). The literal translation, "to crush evil," carries
with it very deep meaning and significance, especially when
viewed in a historical and political context. We've been able
to trace the ancestral roots of the Pattakos family as far back
as 914 AD, during the Byzantine Empire. Along the way, we
also found a long line of family members who had left their
indelible marks on and influenced Greek history in extraordinary and heroic ways.*

In an encyclopedic work, History of Sfakiá, *or a Part
of Cretan History,* published in 1877, we learned that the
Pattakos family was one of the original five families who had
settled in the famous Sfakiá region of Crete. Sfakiá is a rugged and mountainous area in the southwestern part of the
island and, importantly, is considered to be one of the few
places in Greece to never have been fully occupied by foreign
powers. To this day, the legendary Sfakians, like the Spartans, are well-known for their fearless, rebellious, fierce war-
rior spirit. How and why the Pattakos family originally came
to Crete is a story made of the stuff of Homer's legends.*

"Do you know the story of the Seven Brothers?" asked one of our relatives as we sat down to share a delicious Cretan meal. Although we had heard the story many times before, we were eager to hear yet another version.

"Please, tell us," we replied, and so began the story.

Sometime around the Ottoman Turkish conquest, and fall of Constantinople in 1453, members of the Pattakos family moved from Constantinople to Imbros, the largest island and westernmost point of what is now Turkey. Until this time, the entire region of Asia Minor had been largely a Greek settlement and the Greeks uncompromisingly resisted the Ottoman takeover. Because members of the Pattakos family were known to be leaders of the opposition, the impending threat of Turkish oppression eventually forced them to leave for Imbros where they intended to live freely and continue fearlessly to plot against their intruders.

Unfortunately, the move to the island of Imbros didn't fare well for the Pattakos family. Among the members of this proud and freedom-loving clan were seven brothers, all described proudly by our relatives as being tall, handsome, highly intelligent, and fearless! Although the details are a bit sketchy, the seven brothers were sentenced to death by the sultan for a crime that they allegedly had committed—several accounts point to the killing of a Turkish military commander, committed in defense of their honor. However, because the sultana was charmed by the seven brothers, she convinced her husband, the sultan, to grant them a pardon, which also included a provision that forced them to leave Imbros for Crete to live in exile. Because they were freedom fighters at heart, and because of the potential revolutionary threat they posed if they were near their fellow Greeks, the conditions of their exile required the seven brothers to settle on the southern, most uninhabited part of Crete—the region known as Sfakiá. And it was here, in the rugged and mountainous terrain, where the seven brothers founded and named the village of Imbros, one of Crete's highest villages, to commemorate the island from which they first came.

Because the seven brothers were brave and managed many times to save the area from enemies, the name Pattakos became well-known and a symbol of fearlessness and courage. In Imbros today, there is even a family well that bears the name: "The well of the seven brothers!" This well was used throughout the centuries for more than storing water. In fact, the well became a secret place for the villagers and residents in the surrounding area to store weapons in during their hard-fought struggles for freedom against oppression from foreign powers. Since possessing weapons was strictly forbidden by their oppressors (an offense punishable by death), the well allowed the Sfakians to store weapons out of sight by day, and retrieve them for good use in the resistance against occupation by night. To be sure, the "well of the seven Pattakos brothers," which, we are proud to say, we've seen with our very own eyes, is an important and meaningful part of Cretan and Greek history. And the intriguing story behind it offers a great example of how the Greeks embraced fearlessness even in the midst of imminent danger and against overwhelming odds.

Thousands of years ago, the Greeks lived in fear. Unable to understand the natural phenomena that surrounded them in daily life, such as storms, the seasons, and childbirth, they invented elaborate stories of supernatural gods and goddesses to help them calm their fears. Zeus became the king of the gods, responsible for the sky, weather, thunder, and lightning, as well as law and order; Poseidon became the god of the sea; Hades, the god of the dead and the underworld; Hera, the goddess of marriage and childbirth; Hestia, the goddess of hearth and home; Demeter, the goddess of agriculture and the harvest; and so on. The Greeks believed the gods and goddesses would protect them from harm, ensure bountiful harvests, and make their lives a little easier.

Soon the Greeks began to live in fear of the gods, thinking that if they angered the gods, the gods would use their powers to punish them. The Greeks tried to appease the gods through offerings, prayers, rituals, and festivals. Over time, however, encouraged by the Greek philosophers, the Greeks began to ask more questions about their world. By discussing and thinking about the patterns they observed that were occurring naturally in their surroundings, their fear of the world, and of the gods, began to diminish.

"Fear is pain arising from the anticipation of evil."
—ARISTOTLE

The Greek word "phobos," from which the word "phobia" is derived, means fear. A phobia is a fear or intense dislike for something. Many of the words used to describe our fears have been derived from the Greek language. For example, agoraphobia contains the root word "agora," Greek for marketplace, and is the abnormal fear that is characterized by the avoidance of open or public places. Xenophobia contains the Greek root word "xenos," meaning "stranger," and is the fear of strangers or things that are foreign. Interestingly, ergophobia is derived from the Greek word "ergon," meaning "work," and is defined as "the fear of or aversion to work"!

More common phobias include our *fear of success* ("Am I as good as they think I am?"), *fear of failure* ("Will I make a mistake?"), *fear of rejection* ("Will I be respected?"), *fear of loss* ("Will I lose my looks, love, job, or money?"), *fear of change*, and, ultimately, *fear of the unknown*, including death.

EMBRACE *APHOBIA*

🏛 *"To him who is afraid, everything rustles."*
—SOPHOCLES

Many people are afraid to admit they have fears! They may appear arrogant, but behind this facade is a deep sense of fear, including the fear of revealing to others who they truly are. This fear may have stemmed from experiences in the past when they encountered excessive criticism or rejection and were unable to express themselves fully. This fear may have been formed in early childhood when they were taught to be extra careful in life, to hide their mistakes, and to never show vulnerability . . . or alternatively, they may have been taught to be suspicious of the world; taught to believe that the world is limited and that there never *was* or never *will be* enough money, support, or love. By repeating limiting beliefs and behaviors learned in the past, the cycle of fear continues. These unresolved fears from the past are the causes of many forms of anxiety, aggression, depression, addiction, and illness.

Having too many fears and self-doubts paralyzes our growth and blocks us from living our lives to the fullest. Having too many fears zaps our energy and creates unnecessary drama and tension. By giving into our fears, we are allowing something outside of us to have more power over us than we believe we have ourselves.

If we have things (money, job, relationship, etc.), we may be afraid of losing them. Alternatively, if we don't have these things, we may believe we will not get them in the future. We become stuck in our fear, believing that the future will not be any better than the present. We can list many reasons for not moving forward—our past, our family, our lack of connections, our limited education, our neighborhood, our weight, and even the current economic crisis—to rationalize and, by implication, justify our predicament.

189

Paradoxically, due to the law of attraction, our worst fears often become self-fulfilling prophecies.

While in Greece, some people shared that they were living meaningful lives, while others told us that the fear and anxiety associated with not having enough money (for food, shelter, medicine, expenses, education, retirement, or even for entrepreneurial ventures) were the reasons that they could not move forward and live their life with purpose and meaning. While the source of some of their fears definitely could have been grounded in the *reality* of the economic crisis, others were merely perceived fears or threats created in their *imaginations*. It is important to distinguish between the two.

> *"It is better for you to be free of fear lying upon a pallet, than to have a golden couch and a rich table and be full of trouble."*
> —Epicurus

Trust

We all have fears. When we live in fear, it's like living in a thick cloud of fog unable to see clearly. When we lift this cloud, when we address our fears, we are able to see more opportunities and discover more meaning in our lives.

The opposite of phobia is "aphobia," a Greek word meaning "to be without fear." Aphobia begins with trust—trust in ourselves, trust in others, and trust in the universe.

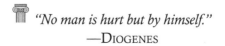

> *"No man is hurt but by himself."*
> —Diogenes

Trust Yourself

"I am seventy-seven. I am very wise!" exclaimed YiaYia Maria in her usual magical way. YiaYia Maria knows that trusting herself is one of the secrets to living a life of meaning. YiaYia Maria also knows that not everyone has this type of trust. Some look to others for their opinions and approval instead of relying on their own. Some compare themselves to others instead of being proud of their own talents and accomplishments. Some choose the path of others instead of forging their own path, effectively putting more faith in others than in themselves.

But there comes a point in all our lives when we must choose to stop relying on others and surrender to ourselves, to trust *in* ourselves and in our intuition or sense of "inner knowing." There comes a time when we have to start to live life from the *inside out*, not from the outside in. There comes a point when we have to stop listening to the negative voices that echo in our heads, telling us that we might be wrong, that we might not be perfect, and begin to accept who we truly are and believe that we can achieve what we really want in life.

There also comes a point in life when we have to realize that what happened in the past is over. The only way the past can continue to influence or harm us is if we continue to bring the events of the past into our present day. We must focus on healing our wounds from the past so that it becomes impossible for anyone to trigger a negative response from us related to our past experiences. We must focus on learning from the past so that we do not repeat the same mistakes or patterns, and so that we grow and develop from what we have learned. As Socrates taught us, there are multiple interpretations for any situation. But until we are willing and able to address the drama from the past, we will continue to relive it in the present and in the future. The bottom line is that in order to move our lives forward, we have to deal with it.

The burdens of our lives are our own creations, or at least are co-created with others. Although we can't always choose our external circumstances, we are 100 percent responsible for how we *respond* to them. We have the power to control our own thoughts and choose our own attitudes. In the end, we are the masters of our fears, our thoughts, and our actions.

Life flows through us. Life brings good things and life brings not-so-good things. We must trust in our ability to know how to live in this flow.

Trust Others

When we trust ourselves, others will begin to trust us and we, in turn, will be able to trust them. When we don't trust others, be they people in our personal lives or at work, we are, in essence, separating ourselves from them. We are living and working from a place of fear, insecurity, and power, not from a place of trust, love, and meaning. The main reasons for the lack of motivation and engagement, especially in the workplace, are that people don't trust one another; they don't trust that they will be supported and understood; and they don't trust that their work really matters, has deep meaning, or is contributing to the greater good. These factors affect not only the organization's bottom line but also the overall meaning of each employee's work and personal life.

When we separate ourselves from others, more often than not we do so out of fear—of being rejected, of being disrespected, of not being supported. The energy that should be flowing naturally between us is blocked and sometimes even stops flowing all together. Fear leads to disconnection and fragmentation, while trust leads to connection and wholeness.

The ancient Greek philosophers believed that all things are interconnected. Imagine how much more productive all of us could be if we trusted ourselves and others more. Imagine how much better off all of us could be if, like we discussed in chapter three (Connect with the Village), we trusted that others would be there to help us in our time of need, and vice versa. Ultimately, though, we know we can only change ourselves, not others. Instead of worrying so much about how others are treating us, it's up to us to make the first move and extend the olive branch of trust to them.

 "As I watched the seagulls, I thought: 'That's the road to take; find the absolute rhythm and follow it with absolute trust.'"
—NIKOS KAZANTZAKIS

Trust the Universe

Pythagoras believed that all things in the world moved together in a beautiful, orderly way. He believed that the basic building blocks for all natural things were numbers and patterns, arranged in order. He urged us to trust that the universe was in harmony and that the best way to live was to *harmonize* ourselves with the way both the physical and spiritual worlds actually flowed.

 "Nothing occurs at random, but everything for a reason and by necessity."
—LEUCIPPUS

Pythagoras asked us to trust that the world is actually very simple at its core. If we are open to this belief, then connections will happen naturally, without us having to force or manipulate them. Synchronicities will happen whereby we will be guided to meet the person we need to meet or learn what we need to learn. According to Pythagoras and other metaphysicians, opportunities will present themselves if we trust in the universe as the source of true power. If we don't trust that this is so, then we will miss these connections and opportunities, and miss finding the deeper meaning in our lives.

What we *believe* obviously has a huge impact on how we live our lives. If we trust that the world is abundant with all kinds of opportunities and resources, and trust in the power of a generous universe that provides for those who seek them out, then maybe, just maybe, *our* world will open up in ways that might never have seemed possible before!

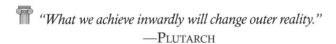 *"What we achieve inwardly will change outer reality."*
—PLUTARCH

Parmenides, another ancient Greek philosopher, believed that to think about something was to give it some form of existence. If we are constantly thinking of negative situations and fears, we are actually manifesting or bringing more of these negative situations and fears into our lives. If we think fear, we get fear. If we focus on problems, we get more problems. From a metaphysical point of view, we attract what we continually think, say, and do. In other words, the universe gives us what we appear to want by allowing us, as Parmenides would say, to bring into existence what is in our consciousness!

Like a mirror, our life is a reflection of our thoughts, attitudes, and actions. If we hope for something but doubt that it will happen, in all likelihood, it won't happen. We get what we tell ourselves over and over again. A negative mind radiates low energy and attracts negativity (that is, inner and outer adversity, such as failure). A positive mind radiates high energy and attracts positivity (that is, inner and outer prosperity, such as success). It is best to focus not on closing doors out of fear, but on opening doors to receive the many blessings and unlimited possibilities that life has to offer.

Courage

On his ten year journey home from Troy to reclaim his rightful place as the king of Ithaka in Homer's Odyssey, *Odysseus encountered many formidable challenges: His ships were blown off course by violent storms; he encountered narcotic lotus plants that left him apathetic toward doing anything; he was captured by the Cyclops; he was enticed by the witch-goddess Circe and the Sirens; he battled the six-headed monster Scylla; and upon arrival in Ithaka, had to fight off the suitors for his wife, Penelope. Throughout his journey, despite being confronted with all these challenges, Odysseus believed things could always be worse!*

In another Greek myth, Jason and his band of heroes, called the Argonauts (named after their ship, Argo*), had to overcome many challenges, such as giants, dragons, crushing rocks, and deception, in their quest for the Golden Fleece.*

These classic stories, like many challenges in our own lives, follow a similar path. First, there is a trigger, an event or crisis that signals the end of a phase and causes or requires a change in our approach. Then, there is the bridge over which we must cross. To cross the bridge, we have to overcome our denial, resistance, and confusion and let go of the old. We have to face and pass through our fears in order to move toward the other side. Finally, we triumph by realizing that we have arrived in a new place with renewed energy and a stronger, more resilient character.

The central theme of all these transformational experiences, be they tales of fiction or stories of real life, is *courage*. The definitions of courage vary from "being without fear" to "confronting or facing fear" in some way. We believe that true courage is not the absence of fear per se, but the willingness and ability to *act* in the face of fear; in other words, to not be stuck by fear but to *move through* the fear.

> *"Brave hearts do not back down."*
> —SOPHOCLES

In *The Odyssey*, Odysseus faced twelve challenges. Many of us have faced at least twelve challenges in our own lives, times when we have been called upon to overcome obstacles and difficulties. It is during these times in life when we have to march right up to what or whom we are afraid of and tackle it or them head on. It is during these times in life when we have to find the courage to move *through* our fears. In doing so, we discover another side of ourselves and gain a deeper sense of faith in ourselves. Many times, after the fact, we come to realize that the challenge was placed in front of us so that we could discover something very important and meaningful about ourselves and our world.

> *"Courage is knowing what not to fear."*
> —PLATO

When our minds are focused on something greater than ourselves, on a goal that is truly meaningful, we are able to summon the courage to move through our fears. Odysseus was focused on the goals of returning to his wife, Penelope, and to his place as the king of Ithaka, while Jason had a goal of obtaining the Golden Fleece so he could reclaim the kingdom of Iolkos. Their burning desire to fulfill these goals was more powerful than their fear. "Where there's a will, there's a way," but Odysseus and Jason, and so many of the Greeks we met along our own journey, clearly demonstrated, "Where there is a purpose, there is a will." When we have a vision of achieving a meaningful goal and we commit to doing whatever it takes to accomplish it, we too will be able to summon the courage and strength to move through our fears and overcome any challenge or discouragement we face along the way.

"He is a man of courage who does not run away, but remains at his post and fights against the enemy."
—SOCRATES

"Those who cannot bravely face danger are the slaves of their attackers."
—ARISTOTLE

"Fortune is not on the side of the faint-hearted."
—SOPHOCLES

It is important to point out that many of the Greek heroes and gods have character flaws or weaknesses of their own. Against the backdrop of these vulnerable "human" attributes, it becomes easier to relate to their personal challenges and adapt their lessons of courage and personal transformation to our own lives.

In Greek mythology, the mother of Achilles dipped him into the river Styx when he was born in an attempt to make him immortal. Unfortunately, the only spot where Achilles was not immortal was the small area on his heel where she had held him when dipping him into the water. Years later, during a battle, Achilles was killed by an arrow shot by Paris, which pierced his vulnerable heel. (Achilles was a hero of the Trojan War and the central character in Homer's Iliad.) Today, we use the term "Achilles' heel" metaphorically to indicate the area where someone (or a group or organization) has a weakness or is vulnerable.

We need to recognize our own Achilles' heels in order to move forward. As Plato taught, "For a man to conquer himself, is the first and noblest of all victories." We need to acknowledge, "It is me who is holding me back, not someone else." Self-confidence is a choice. We can either choose to believe in ourselves or not. When we believe in ourselves, we discover that we had the strength all along to go beyond what we thought were our limits. When we feel good about ourselves, we project this positive energy into the world and the world responds accordingly.

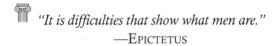 *"It is difficulties that show what men are."*
—EPICTETUS

Odysseus and Jason needed courage to perform their heroic acts, but so too did the Greeks while living through occupations and wars. It is because of this history that many of the Greeks we met on our journey felt confident that they would get through the current economic crisis. "As long as we focus on what's important—food, shelter, our health, relationships, helping others—we will be fine. We will get by," explained our friend Mihalis. "Challenges can either defeat us or make us strong! Challenges test us; we can either retreat in fear or we can rise up. We are like the Minotaur—half man, half bull," he declared, waving his hands with enthusiasm.

When we focus on the difficulties of life and on what's wrong or what's missing, we lose power and energy. When we procrastinate, waiting for the situation to be "right," standing on the sidelines of life, we lose valuable time and experiences. When the Greeks smash plates, they do so to cast away their burdens and to let go of their problems or things standing in their way. They smash plates to symbolize their courage, that they are free, and that they are ready to take on life!

> *"You do not develop courage by being happy in your relationships everyday—you develop it by surviving difficult times and challenging adversity."*
> —EPICURUS

Life, as we all know but sometimes seem to forget, requires patience, perseverance, and courage. On one trip to Greece, we watched in awe as an aging donkey, overladen with a dozen cases of beer strapped onto his back, descended the steep steps along the cliff side of the island of Santorini. Unlike some people who give up just before they reach their goal or lose their balance when things get tough, this donkey dug deep within his soul and, step by step, forced his way through his fears. The donkey proved, without question, that he had both heart and courage by refusing to give up on himself. Neither should we!

> *"The greater the difficulty, the more the glory in surmounting it."*
> —EPICURUS

Throughout our journey, we met Greeks who showed that they were neither timid nor shy, nor were they blocked in their thinking. Consistent with their resilient, defiant spirit, and like the donkey described above, these Greeks displayed an attitude of stubborn determination, heart, and courage. Deep in their souls, they knew that they could, *and always would*, persevere and find a solution to whatever challenges came their way. Their attitude reminded us of the movie *300*, a fictionalized retelling of King Leonidas and his three hundred Spartans at the Battle of Thermopylae (ca 480 BC). This famous last stand by the Spartans has become an eternal symbol of courage against overwhelming odds. When King Leonidas was asked by King Xerxes of Persia to hand over his weapons, Leonidas simply replied, "Come and take them." Spartan courage in the face of pain, danger, and adversity is well-known and universally admired. Another Spartan king, Agis II, who reigned more than fifty years after Leonidas did, is credited by the ancient Greek biographer Plutarch as saying, "The Spartans do not ask how many are the enemy but where are they." To this day, the word "Spartan" conjures up vivid images of courage, uncompromising determination, and relentless self-discipline. In addition, a disciplined Spartan lifestyle emphasizes strength of mind, body, and spirit, and is grounded purposefully in simplicity and frugality.

"Courage is the first of human qualities because it is the quality which guarantees the others."
—ARISTOTLE

It takes courage to realize that situations change, people change. What worked last year might not work this year. But many people fear letting go of "the way we do things around here" to venture into the unknown and try something new. It takes courage to *say* what needs to be said and to *do* what needs to be done. It takes courage to face the criticism that frequently comes with offering new and creative ideas. It takes courage to challenge the status quo, explore new pathways, and expand the boundaries of what is possible. Leaving the crowd, risking separation from the pack, requires deep personal strength and resolve.

Hercules is the Roman name for the divine hero in Greek mythology, Herakles. He was the son of Zeus and half-brother of Perseus. He possessed extraordinary strength, courage, and ingenuity, which he used to overcome many formidable challenges throughout his life. Today we use the descriptive term "Herculean" to refer metaphorically to a large and difficult task or challenge that would require someone with the personal attributes of Hercules to accomplish it.

On every trip to Greece, we witness how finding alternatives, shortcuts, and creative solutions comes naturally for the Greeks. For example, when faced with a busy road between the Blue Palace Resort and the beach, they dug a tunnel *under* the road to allow their customers and staff easy and safe access between the two locations. When mirrors in a bathroom blocked the view of the sea, they installed movable mirrors. When the climb down to the beach was too steep, they installed an elevator.

In a nearby restaurant, when the tables near the sea were full, the waiters offered a table inside "where it isn't too windy," and when those tables were full, they creatively offered a table off to the side "where it is quiet." Every table, in other words, was the *best in the house*—it just depended on your perspective!

Throughout Greece, we witnessed their ability to ask new questions, see new connections, and explore new opportunities. The creative mind and spirit are integral parts of the Greek DNA, inherited from many centuries ago, when they led the world with breakthroughs in many areas. Today, we see this mind at work, courageously maneuvering through the chaos and bureaucracy. "It can be done, we will make it happen. There is always a way." They may be short on financial resources, but they are never short on ingenuity and resourcefulness!

If you love honey, don't be afraid of the bee.
TRADITIONAL VILLAGE WISDOM

Elastikos

To be resilient means to be flexible, capable of adapting to and quickly recovering from change. The Greek origin of this concept is the word "elastikos," from which the English word "elastic" is derived, which refers to the idea that we are able to recover our shape after being stretched!

Thousands of years ago, the Greek philosophers had much to say about change. Some like Pythagoras believed that nothing new really emerges, nothing new ever goes away, and that everything is simply a repetition of the past. Empedocles also believed that everything already exists; it's simply in the process of reorganizing itself into something that appears new! He believed that there was a pattern of repeated actions, when things would come together and unite as one and then fall apart again. This is how new things seem to come into existence.

Heraclitus, who was a contemporary of the Buddha, Lao-tzu, and Confucius, believed the opposite. His famous quote "You can never step into the same river twice" reflects his strong and fundamental belief in the transitory nature of life. In other words, the river where you first set your foot is gone; it is now a different river. The river, like life, is constantly flowing, and to deny this flow is to deny the essential characteristic of life, which is *change*.

Indeed, the nature of life *is* change but we often resist this, wanting things to remain the same, trying to design and control our lives so that change does not happen. We think that if we stay in the same house, work in the same place at the same job, and keep the same friends, we'll be able to avoid having to deal with change. But the status quo is an illusion because, even if we want to stand still, everyone and everything else around us is changing. There is a saying, "If you want things to stay the same, then something is going to have to change!" The sooner we accept and seek to accommodate this basic fact of life—that nothing in life ever really stands still—the more resilient and less stressed we will be!

Life cannot be preprogrammed, for it flows like a river, twisting and turning, changing at different rates, sometimes appearing more stable, while at other times, tossing us around in the turbulent rapids. We can try our best to hold onto the sides of the river of life to resist the flow, dreading or fearing change but, in the end, we know that life requires us to surrender to the forward motion and "go with the flow" of the river.

> *"Make the best use of what is in your power, and take the rest as it happens."*
> —EPICTETUS

Optimistically, Heraclitus also believed that "the sun is new each day." Every day brings us new opportunities to start fresh and change our perspective toward how we might best answer life's call. Difficult times, such as economic crises, droughts, conflicts, etc., will pass eventually and a new day will come that offers the prospect, not simply the hope, of better times. It may rain but the sun always shines again. To paraphrase Heraclitus, no situation is ever permanent. And the concept of resilience—elastikos—demands that we believe this to be the case, for without the prospect of a better tomorrow, our ability to effectively navigate the white water of today will be greatly diminished.

"Nothing in the affairs of men is worthy of great anxiety."
—PLATO

"There is only one way to happiness and that is to cease worrying about things which are beyond the power of our will."
—EPICTETUS

To be truly and radically resilient, we should expect changes in our relationships, finances, health, work, communities, economy, and political system. To be truly and radically resilient, we should recognize what is within and what is outside our power and sphere of influence, so that we don't have a false sense of control over things. Suffering comes from trying to control the uncontrollable and trying to live in a safe, stable world of controlled predictability (our comfort zone). Suffering, in this context, comes from having unrealistic expectations.

We need to have the wisdom to know what we can change and what we cannot. We also need to have insight into what we should change and what we should not. If we have too much fear, or if we are worrying too much, it's a signal that we are trying to control too much of our lives and that we are not in touch with the *meta*physical side of life. If we are trying to (re)create the world as we want it versus dealing with the reality of the world as it is, we will most likely suffer as a result. By the same token, if we avoid trying to find out what really matters to us in life and taking steps to move forward in a meaning-focused direction, ultimately we will suffer as a result. Resilience involves believing that we can make things better for ourselves versus being helpless victims of our circumstances. It also involves assuming personal responsibility for our fate and, at the same time, knowing the limits of our control.

Life, once again, is not about pursuing balance per se; rather, it's about building resilience so that we can deal with the unexpected. It's about being able to bounce back from the disappointments in our life and work. It's about being able to let go of some things in order to let other things happen.

As Epictetus suggested, it is not about what happens to us, but how we react to what happens that really matters. We may not have control over a situation, but we do have control over how we react to it, how we think and feel about it, as well as what we do about it. If we have strength within, we will have more energy to deal with the external world, as opposed to overreacting to everything that happens. All things being equal, the more we are able to observe things happening without absorbing the suffering and negativity around us, the more resilient we will become. The more positive and resilient the people with whom we associate and surround ourselves, the more resilient we will become. Moreover, the more variety and diversity we have in our lives, the better, so that, if one relationship or job doesn't pan out, we know that we are resilient and have other options.

Life, in the big picture, is not about being content. Life is dynamic, a flow of energy much like a river; as such, it is meant to be lived to the fullest. Being content is like putting one's car into neutral and sitting back. Sooner or later, the car comes to a stop since it no longer has any more gas to keep going, let alone to take us, ideally, where we'd like to go!

A life well-lived and purpose-driven, as opposed to one that is running on empty, is one of adventure and based on continuous learning and growth—that is, constantly moving toward a new and meaningful goal. A life well-lived and purpose-driven is one in which we know that we have the resilience to cope with whatever life throws at us. At the same time, we acknowledge that life is a blessing and should never be taken for granted. Indeed, whatever our personal circumstances may be, we appreciate, like the Greek hero Odysseus, that it could always be worse!

*As a **tribute to all** the wonderful Greek fishermen we met on our journey, here are a few words of wisdom to help us build elastikos, or resilience, in our lives:*

- *Respect that life, like the sea, is always changing and that we cannot control these changes.*
- *Stay buoyant and find the inner strength to weather the unpredictable storms of life.*
- *Believe that the new day, just like the tide, will bring in good things and wash away bad things.*
- *Be patient. We cannot rush life, just like we cannot rush the fish. Things of quality take time.*
- *Realize that tension on our line is good, it means there is life.*
- *Know that there are always more fish in the sea, more options than we can see right now.*
- *Have courage. Sometimes we have to sail against the wind and chart our own course.*

- *Remember we can only see the surface of the sea (or of issues), which is only a very small part of what lies beneath.*

- *Take time to gather with others to discuss the day and give thanks for the catch.*

- *Wear our fisherman cap (with The OPA! Way logo) as an inspirational symbol of the freedom of the sea and our courage to navigate the adventures of life.*

Summary

Aphobia means being without fear. Just as the ancient Greeks shifted from fear to belief in their own abilities, we can also shift from our fear of the unknown to a clearer understanding of the opportunities we have to create a life of joy and meaning. But when our fear is stronger than our faith, we start to question the meaning of things, including the meaning of our life. When we worry, it's a signal that we've lost the connection to meaning. On the other hand, when we trust, we are connected to meaning. We then realize that we don't have to hold on to everything so tightly— we can let go and see life as an exciting adventure and a celebration to be fully experienced, not something only to be endured or controlled.

We all face many challenges in life; however, like the Greek heroes Odysseus and Jason, we also have the opportunity to summon courage—the ability to move through our fears—in the face of them. In this connection, we all have the capacity to embrace and develop elastikos and demonstrate that we can be flexible, adaptive, and resilient no matter what our personal circumstances may be. And as we meaningfully engage our spirits, minds, and bodies, we'll come to realize that the changes we are waiting for are those that *we*, as truly self-empowered human beings, will make happen. Embracing aphobia means that we are always learning and growing, as well as always expressing who we truly are.

OPA! AFFIRMATION

I find joy and meaning in my life when I embrace life with aphobia.

11

Embrace *Well-Being*

After descending the many winding steps down the hillside in Oia, Santorini, we arrived at the local taverna so highly recommended by our Greek friends. *A charming table for two overlooking the bay awaited us. "Yiasas," we said in unison to the young waiter who welcomed us. After settling in with the customary glass of wine, olives, and freshly baked bread, we appreciated the opportunity to let time slip away as we watched the small fishing boats bouncing in the water before us.*

"Now this is living," proclaimed Alex. "Don't you feel relaxed? Don't you feel healthy? The fresh air, the sea, the food!" he continued as he reached for a piece of fish, masterly prepared and served, swimming in olive oil on the large white platter that had been placed before us.

"Yes, I do feel healthier. Remember when YiaYia Georgina told us about the people she sees in the big city— that they look gray and so tired, so unhealthy?"

We remembered YiaYia's simple wisdom: You are healthy if you have good color in your face. You are unhealthy if you look gray, drained of color. We also remembered that some people believe that if your tongue is pink, you are healthy, but if your tongue is white or gray, you are unhealthy . . . or if your eyes are clear white you are healthy, but if they are yellowed or pink, you are unhealthy. Such simple signs . . .

We found it interesting that many of the Greeks we had met were so focused on their health. We recalled meeting Krystoula one day, in a knife shop in Rethymno. When we said that perhaps one day her young son, Giorgos, would be a famous gymnast and go to the Olympic Games, she simply replied, "We have our health, we only need our health." So many of the Greeks we spoke with about the economic crisis shared a similar perspective, "I have my health so I am good. As long as we are healthy, we can make our way through this." As we continued our dinner, watching the last remnants of the sun set on the horizon, we began to realize what the Greeks have known for thousands of years—that keeping a positive attitude toward our own well-being must be a priority.

Thousands of years ago, many people believed the gods *sent* as well as *cured* illnesses. They retreated to the sanctuaries dedicated to the god of healing, Asklepios, son of the god Apollo, to be healed. Some say Alcmaeon, who lived in the fifth century BC, was the real father of medicine because he was the first to believe that the responsibility for health and healing lay not with the gods but with mankind. He is believed to be the first to state that one's nutrition, lifestyle, and environment affected one's health. He is also believed to be the first to dissect the human body, looking for clues to illness and disease. Alcmaeon is not nearly as well-known as Hippocrates.

Hippocrates is famous for his work discovering the connection between health and lifestyle. His was a holistic approach to well-being: He asked his patients about their emotions, fears, dreams, sleeping patterns, diets, the location of their homes, etc., while he examined their bodies, especially their bodily fluids, for clues about their overall health. He observed nature, especially the seasons and their effect on the body, to discover causes of illnesses. His scientific observations, analysis, and writings laid the foundation for modern medicine. The "Oath of Hippocrates," or Hippocratic oath, embodies the ethics and ideals of Hippocrates and urges physicians to maintain ethical standards by swearing respect for others and for life in general. "Do no harm," is one of its most famous ideas.

Following the groundwork laid by Hippocrates, Aristotle observed and analyzed nature for the causes of disease, although he also believed that well-being was a combination of the physical and *meta*physical, that is, beyond the physical or spiritual, elements. Although some people believe our spirits, minds, and bodies are all separate, the ancient Greeks and many of us today strongly believe that these things are interconnected and therefore interdependent—each affects the other.

Energy

Life is about energy—the flow of energy both within us, and between us and others.

Energy flows freely within us when our heart, lungs, blood circulation, and digestive systems are all working in harmony. But when our breathing is shallow, when our hearts are weak, or when our digestion is poor, our energy flow is blocked. Poor nutrition and inactivity can lead to spikes in our blood sugar and insulin levels, inflammation and damaged cells, mood swings, and weight gain. Things fall out of balance and disease, or "dis-ease," begins.

The condition of the body can be an expression of the spirit within. Thoughts and emotions can work to promote good health by giving us energy or can, conversely, make us sick by blocking the flow of energy. When we are engaged in activities we enjoy, when we feel that we matter, and when we have an optimistic, positive attitude, we feel more energetic. Conversely, we feel drained of energy when we are engaged in activities that are meaningless to us or feel that we are not living authentically; when we are overwhelmed with anxiety, excessive worry, anger, and resentment; when we feel that we lack control over our lives; or when we complain incessantly and have a negative attitude.

When we resist what is and what is supposed to be, or we repress feelings and unresolved emotions, we interrupt the flow of energy. These energy blockages eventually show up in some form as illness. Everything on some level is connected. We cannot ignore or discount problems in one area of our lives for they will show up in another. Our overall state of well-being rests on us having a strong spirit, strong mind, and strong body—they cannot be separated. (We often hear the phrase "body, mind, and spirit." However, we believe that the phrase is backward: It should be "spirit, mind, and body," because if we don't engage the spirit first, then the mind [emotions, thoughts] and the body [action, behaviors] will be weak. Spirit gives energy and power to our desires and intentions, as well as encourages us to take action.)

We have heard that in the United States, more heart attacks occur on Mondays than any other day of the week. How would the body know it was Monday, if it wasn't for the mind reacting to the stresses associated with the start of the work week, affecting the health of the overall body?

Stress levels are on the rise in every country. Stress can be real or perceived. It's our perception of any given situation and our reaction to this perception that causes most of the stress in our lives. If we view our workplace as being toxic or other people as being hostile, or if we fear that there are too many demands on us and we lack control over how we can deal with these demands, we trigger tension and anxiety in ourselves. If we always think that the world is falling apart, we can trigger even more anxiety. Stress causes our bodies to react in some way.

While a certain level of stress is healthy, which endocrinologist Hans Selye called "eustress" (from the Greek, meaning "good stress"), its opposite, "distress," is what is normally associated with the negative and unhealthy side of stress. Too much of any kind of stress can lead to a decrease in our ability to think and perform. When we are stressed, the flow of energy in our bodies is interrupted, our bodies go into panic mode and tighten, we breathe faster, and our nerve centers go on alert, which affects the circulation of blood. In response to stress, our bodies also release adrenalin and hormones (CRH, ACTH, and cortisol), which, at too-high levels and for prolonged periods, can have serious negative effects on our health and well-being. Our bodies have to fight to maintain equilibrium. If we put ourselves into stressful situations (real or perceived) and put our bodies through this reaction too often, we risk damage to our bodies. We are not built to stay in highly stressful situations for long periods of time. We need to allow our bodies the time to rest and recover from stress before the next stress episode occurs.

To be sure, some illnesses are caused by genetics, but some are caused by our poor lifestyles, including chronic stress and blocked energy. Our bodies give us warning signs that we are out of alignment or in need of repair just like our car knocks or makes funny noises, signaling that it is time to bring it in for service. These physical aches and pains tell us to pay attention. If we ignore these signs, the effects of prolonged stress accumulate and lead to poor health.

Perhaps Americans are in denial about how unhealthy we have become. The United States spends close to 20 percent of its gross domestic product (GDP), or about $2 trillion, on health care, yet its citizens suffer from very high rates of obesity, diabetes, heart disease, cancer, addictions, and depression. The majority of visits to the family doctor are to address some stress-related symptoms, such as anxiety, insomnia, arthritis, hypertension, depression, digestive issues, etc. For various reasons, physicians today have little time to see each patient and even less time to ask about lifestyle or stress and the broader connection between the spirit, mind, and body. Instead, more often than not, they are forced to focus primarily on relieving symptoms and managing diseases quickly through drugs or surgery.

Over 90 percent of our health care budgets are spent on treatment versus prevention. If stage 1 is being healthy, stage 2 is having stress and blocked energy, and stage 3 is illness, most people wait until they are in stage 3 to react and then want quick fixes for their illnesses. If we focused on prevention of illness and, in particular, on stages 1 and 2, we would not only be healthier (individually and as a nation), we would save billions of dollars in health care costs. Just as we actively prevent car accidents by encouraging people to take driver's education classes, and just as we brush our teeth to prevent cavities, we can learn to take a more proactive approach to our general health and well-being by focusing on the prevention of illness.

The villagers in Greece, like their ancestors, take a holistic approach to their well-being. This approach, which gives priority to prevention over treatment, acknowledges that resilience to stress and having a positive attitude and healthy lifestyle, including diet and activities, all contribute in very meaningful ways to the body's infinite capacity to become healthier and heal itself. We need to become more aware of how much we can do for our health by improving our attitude toward life and work; making healthier lifestyle choices, including the type and quantity of food we eat; and committing authentically to finding harmony in spirit, mind, and body.

Moderation

Two-thirds of Americans are either overweight or obese! We are not only eating too much but also eating too much of the wrong foods. In our "super size" culture, some people are eating twice the calories recommended for them on a daily basis. Overeating is literally making us sick. Our bodies are having a difficult time processing both the quantity of food and the artificial chemicals and other ingredients found in many of our processed foods.

The Greek word "pleonexia" means "love of more and more." Food, in particular, is readily accessible so we can snack at any time. Instead of indulging on special feast days, *every* day becomes a feast day. The design of food and its packaging makes eating exciting and hypnotically addictive, so we eat the food no matter what the nutritional value of it may be. We like and become accustomed to the taste of salt and sugar and soon want more. The large portions, either in jumbo snack packages or in restaurants, are placed in front of us so we eat everything. We eat and eat and still feel hungry. We drink high-calorie drinks instead of zero-calorie water. We turn to food when we feel stressed or when life is difficult, seeking in vain to reward ourselves with it or make ourselves feel better about a certain situation. We use food to ignore unresolved emotional issues or escape from boredom. We eat too much food compared to the amount of movement we do on a daily basis, and it shows in more ways than one. Instead of eating five hundred calories and working off five hundred calories, we eat *more* and exercise *less*. And then we wake up and wonder why we don't feel well!

"Nothing in excess" is a quote inscribed in the temple of Apollo at Delphi that is attributed to one or more of the Seven Sages of Greece, including Chilon, Cleobulus, and Solon. With the freedom to eat whatever we want also comes the responsibility to eat properly and according to nature.

Aristotle believed that self-control is "the ability to restrain desire by reason." He believed that if we couldn't control our desires, we were nothing more than animals. Aristotle references the Greek word "enkrateia," meaning inner strength or self-discipline, as support for his views on moderation. He advised us to find a balance, which is between the extremes of too much food (excess) and too little food (deficiency). We must observe this "golden mean" or things fall out of balance and our overall health and well-being suffer.

We shouldn't feel obligated to finish what's on our plates! If the plate is large and piled high with food, we need to make the extra effort not to overeat. We need to voluntarily decrease our portion sizes. Greeks serve food on large platters that are shared by a whole group, and individuals then use small plates to sample a little of everything. Outside of meals, Greeks only eat *mezes* or *mezedes*, small snacks, such as olives, cheese, and vegetables enjoyed during the day.

Epicurus warned us to think of the long-term implications of our actions and forgo the pursuit of pleasure in the short term. He believed short-term pleasures (like eating lots of food or unhealthy food) weren't worth having if they led to greater pain (like feeling guilty or sick) in the future.

🏛 *"One should eat to live, not live to eat."*
　　　　　—Socrates

Throughout Greece we encountered people who were partaking in the ritual of fasting, or voluntarily not eating certain foods, at specified times during the year: "No meat, eggs, or dairy products for us this week." Some Greeks spend almost half the year engaged in some sort of fast. When they eliminate meat from their diet, they become part or "quasi" vegetarian by default. During these times, they turn to their traditional plant-based diet, eating lots of fruits, vegetables, and beans. They firmly believe that the benefits of fasting are physical as well as psychological and spiritual in nature. By denying themselves certain foods, they not only cleanse their bodies but test their willpower and self-control, and prepare themselves for the future (believing that self-discipline is the key to future success). They also know that they will appreciate the food they've been missing even more when they eat it later on.

When not fasting, some say breakfast is the most important meal of the day, but that depends on what it is. If breakfast consists of sugary processed cereals or chocolate donuts, it could cause a blood sugar spike and then a crash by mid-morning. Many Greeks we met ate only a very light breakfast, consisting of whole grain toast, honey, olives, and perhaps a bit of fruit. When they ate is also important. The villagers traditionally would rise at dawn and have only a drink (perhaps hot lemon water or herbal tea, which helped cleanse the digestive system) before they started their morning chores. A few hours later, they would return and have a light meal. This allowed their system a chance to cleanse itself of toxins or waste as well as to wake up before putting it to work. Exercising or moving on an empty stomach early in the morning helps with the fat-burning process before the body shifts to processing food. This tradition makes a mid-morning meal, not an early breakfast, the most important meal of the day!

The OPA! Way Lifestyle

We believe the origin of the word "medicine" has roots in the Greek language. The first part, "*medi,*" refers to "median," "middle" or "center." The second part, "*kine,*" refers to "move" or "to set in movement," as it appears in the word "kinetic." (There is no "c" in the Greek alphabet.) Thus, the concept of medicine can be interpreted as "to move to the center" or to return to the center where our body is in a state of equilibrium or total health.

When we eat to excess, when we eat too many foods that have been processed or that contain too much saturated fat or sugar, when we sit idle, when we subject our bodies to prolonged periods of stress, or when we don't get adequate sleep—we are taking ourselves away from our center. We need some form of medicine or movement to take us back toward the center. Sometimes our bodies should take advantage of and need intervention from modern science and pharmaceuticals, but there are many natural things we can do to help ourselves *move toward the center.* This can be achieved by following The OPA Way! Lifestyle, a holistic, comprehensive approach to well-being, which we review in this chapter.

"The part can never be well unless the whole is well."
—PLATO

The OPA Way! Lifestyle includes all aspects of well-being, such as attitude, activity, and diet. Interestingly, the Greek word, "diaita," means "way of life" or "way of living," but over the years it has been translated into the word "diet," which is narrowly defined as the foods and drinks we consume. The common approach to health today is to compartmentalize its various aspects (diet or exercise) rather than look at them holistically. Our very unique, multilevel pyramid approach to well-being is *lifestyle*centric, not foodcentric. It reinforces the key choices we need to make to live a life full of energy and meaning. It is not just about living longer, it is about living better.

THE OPA! WAY® LIFESTYLE

Others, Purpose, and Attitude

We begin at the base of The OPA! Way Lifestyle pyramid with Others, Purpose, and Attitude (OPA!) as described in the previous chapters of this book.

> **Others:** The health benefits of connecting meaningfully with others are well-known. We need to take time to eat and drink with others. It is rare in Greece to

see people eating and drinking while walking down a street. Instead, they gather around a table to share in conversation and laughter, create a sense of community, and build awareness of interdependency and belonging. Feeling connected and sharing our daily challenges gives us energy and helps alleviate stress. Loneliness, feeling isolated or separated from others, depletes our energy and can lead to depression and illness. Epicurus also taught us that whom we eat with is as important as what we eat. It is important to associate with others who embrace health and well-being, as their attitudes and habits tend to influence our own.

Purpose: Lack of purpose, whether caused by boredom, unemployment, or not knowing what we want next in our life, can drain our energy. When we are living a life or working at a job that doesn't help us find deeper meaning and fulfillment, our well-being suffers as a result. Helping others, extending beyond ourselves in our work and in our personal lives, and feeling valued and appreciated for who we are and what we do, are all good for our overall health and well-being. Having purpose nourishes our spirits and gives us the energy we need to achieve our highest potential and live a life full of meaning.

Attitude: When people say they are tired, they may not just be tired physically but also may be "tired in spirit"—zapped of energy due to untreated or unexpressed emotional pain. Having a pessimistic attitude, anxiety, and depression all block the flow of energy and can create disease, as well as exacerbate preexisting conditions. Our attitudes play a big role in our health, including the prevention of and recovery from illness. In order to fully heal our bodies, we must first heal our minds and spirits. Being optimistic, believing that we are resilient and can deal with challenges and stress, and expressing ourselves authentically, can all lead to stronger immune systems, stronger hearts, and higher states of well-being.

Rejuvenation

The ancient Greek sanctuaries dedicated to Asklepios used many methods for rejuvenating the spirit, mind, and body, such as mountain air, ample sunlight, relaxation, music, water, deep sleep, and proper nutrition, including the use of medicinal herbs. Today, we see Greece (or as we refer to it, "one big spa"!) as the best place for health and wellness. The fresh air, sunshine, blue water, healthy food, and kindhearted, hospitable people all contribute to replenishing our souls, boosting our energy, and promoting our health and well-being.

The Greek word for rejuvenation is "ksananeoma," which loosely means "again a new me!" The body, mind, and spirit have a large capacity for healing and finding their way back to the center. The challenge for many of us, however, is that we have never been taught how to intentionally renew ourselves; or if we do know how, we tend to overlook this knowledge or fail to put it into practice when life gets busy.

> **Rest:** Weekends in America used to represent time to recharge, but now they are often filled with chores or work. Vacations used to last two weeks, but now the average vacation is just a few days and often overscheduled with activities. Despite this, we need more rest today than we did ten or twenty years ago because we are facing an avalanche of information to process, as well as too much change. We need time to process all the stimuli, and time to withdraw to gather strength. Indeed, finding the time and creating opportunities to unplug and recharge ourselves is more important than ever. The Greeks we met understand the need for rest, reflection, and self-nourishment.

They follow their natural biorhythms, take rest periods throughout the day, and welcome solitude as a chance to refuel.

Breath: A fundamental method for rejuvenation is breathing properly. Breathing is such a natural part of our lives but we don't realize that we often hold our breath or forget to breathe, especially in stressful situations. When we hunch over a desk or computer, we squeeze our solar plexus, which is the central energy point of the body, and inhibit the full flow of oxygen. Proper breathing fills our lungs with air and revitalizes the body with life energy. In order to maximize our well-being, we also need to slow down our breathing several times as day, thereby releasing tension and stress and lowering our heart rates.

Sleep: The Greek god of sleep is Hypnos, from which we derive the words "hypnosis" and "hypnotherapy." Hippocrates believed in the power of analyzing people's sleep patterns and their dreams in order to fully understand a person's total health and state of well-being. We need a good night's sleep in order to repair our immune systems and replenish our energy levels. However, many people have trouble falling asleep or staying asleep. Insomnia is one of the main symptoms of stress. If we do not get a proper night's sleep, the stress creates changes in our blood sugar and raises the level of cortisol (known as the stress hormone) in our bodies, which, among other things, can lead to more fat deposits and adverse effects on our health. Like the ancient Greeks who visited the sanctuaries of Asklepios for peace and quiet, ideally we need to re-create this sense of calm every night by not dwelling on the tasks we must do or situations that make us tense or angry. Instead, we should think of things for which we are grateful.

Water: Thales believed that all life originated from water. His belief that water is the basis for all life was embraced by many Greeks, including Hippocrates. They endorsed the healing power of water and encouraged others to visit the sea, springs, and baths. Water therapy, called thalassotherapy (associated with Thales and the Greek word for sea, "thalassa"), uses seawater and products such as seaweed to reduce inflammation and enhance circulation in the body while reenergizing the skin. Enjoying a long, hot, relaxing bath has more healing power than taking a quick shower does.

"Music gives a soul to the universe, wings to the mind, flight to the imagination, and life to everything."
—PLATO

Music: For the ancient Greeks, music was also used for healing: as a way to relax, take the mind off stressors, and access the metaphysical level of our well-being. They believed that the body was more likely to be healed if it was relaxed and rejuvenated. Pythagoras believed that music had special power over our souls. Its harmony and vibration, that is, harmonics and resonance properties, have the power to influence our emotions, minds, and bodies, and helps to reenergize us and create a stronger sense of well-being. On our odyssey, we had the great fortune to meet Giorgos Papalexakis in Rethymno, Crete, who has become famous as a maker of the Cretan lyre, a pear-shaped, three-stringed bowed musical instrument. "Every day, I swim in the sea, do gymnastics, and make lyre," Giorgos told us, adding with hungry enthusiasm, "Music feeds my spirit."

To be sure, we would be remiss if we didn't mention that laughter and sex, two favorite Greek pastimes, also relieve tension and help with relaxation and rejuvenation!

223

Movement

When in Greece, we would see many villagers walking throughout the village, doing chores, helping neighbors, and preparing food for daily meals—all of which require movement and effort. We saw older men walking with their hands clasped behind their backs, opening up their chests and taking in deep breaths. In the evening, we saw many villagers out for a stroll, clearing their minds and relieving stress at the end of the day so they could sleep better. Even in Athens, we had to admire the *yiayia* (grandmother) who climbed the two sets of stairs, from the subway to the street, while we took the escalator!

Walking is an integral part of Greek culture. Thousands of years earlier, Aristotle encouraged his students to walk with him as they listened to him philosophize about life. He founded the Peripatetic School of philosophy and became known as a "Peripatetic lecturer" because he *walked* as he taught (from the Greek word "peripato," meaning "to walk" or "to take for a walk").

 *"Do not consider painful what is good for you."*
—EURIPIDES

Movement reenergizes us, strengthens the elasticity of our muscles, and boosts the flow of oxygen and blood throughout our bodies, especially to our brains, lungs, and heart. Movement helps move the fluids and toxins in our body so they don't just sit there and cause disease. Movement is especially important as we age and when we are under stress or depressed. Generally speaking, when we move, we strengthen our immune systems so that our bodies can withstand the stresses we put on them. If we are inactive, our immune systems may be weaker, and our bodies may be less resilient and more vulnerable to illnesses, including Type 2 diabetes and heart disease.

Outdoors

There are two worlds: the world made by human beings and the world of nature. Bombarded by technology, cars, pollution, processed foods, computers, and the stress of work, we can turn to nature and the great outdoors to help heal us. A simple solution is to bring nature into our homes and workplaces with bright colors, plants and flowers, photos or artwork depicting nature, and natural food. A more desirable solution is for us to spend time *in nature* as often as possible. We are very fortunate to be able to connect with nature on a regular basis in both Santa Fe, New Mexico, USA, and in Crete, Greece. Both are places designed by Mother Nature for healing our spirits, minds, and bodies!

Poor health can result from being caught up in the chaos of big-city living and demanding workplaces, while good health can result from being in calm, peaceful, healing environments. Hippocrates and Asklepios believed that our geographic location can affect our health and took this view into account when offering advice on how best to advance health and well-being. Their spas and sanctuaries, for instance, were located away from the dirt and stress of the big cities. They recommended getting plenty of natural light and sunshine, which boosts the immune system with vitamin D. As one villager told us, "A person not seen by the sun is seen by the doctor!"

During our visits to YiaYia Maria's house, we noticed that she avoided using chemical-based household and personal care products. Chemicals from these products made in the lab may accumulate in the cells of our bodies and may cause skin irritations, allergies, or even more serious illnesses. Her natural home, of course, also did not have any paints or carpets with chemical ingredients that could adversely affect her clean, fresh air!

Moderation and Fasting

This part of The OPA! Way Lifestyle pyramid was discussed earlier in this chapter.

The Food Portion of The OPA! Way Lifestyle

Kali orexi is the Greek expression for "good appetite." From the Greek word "orexi," we derive the word "anorexia," which means "low or no appetite" or, on an even deeper level, means "low or depressed spirit."

What we choose to eat, in large part, determines our level of energy and our state of well-being. If we feel sluggish and tired, if we are sick or have Type 2 diabetes or heart problems, we need to review carefully what we have eaten. Did we eat food that was nutritious and should heal or otherwise benefit our body, or did we eat poor quality food as filler or for pleasure or to alleviate boredom and stress?

> *"Let your food be your medicine."*
> —HIPPOCRATES

The unexamined food is not worth eating! The foods we choose to eat play a major role in the early prevention of disease. If we choose to eat low quality food, what one of our Greek cousins, Elsa, calls "plastic food," we may make ourselves sick. Eating good quality food is especially important as we age; younger bodies can bounce back more easily, but as we age, the body, especially our digestive tract, is less resilient and more sensitive to what is ingested. The heart and brain also need nutritious food in order to function properly. Too much sugar, salt, and saturated fat damages the body and may lead to illness and depression. We can either choose to pay up front for high quality food or we can pay later on with expensive, often painful health care treatments!

In Greece, food is a powerful thread that connects all Greeks to the land, to their roots, and to one another. Eating healthy food and taking good care of oneself is part of the traditional Greek culture. Following long-standing tradition and cultural practice, the Greek diet, the foundation of the Mediterranean Diet, makes magic with a few basic, high quality ingredients found in nature. As many Greeks very wisely told us, "We know what we are eating."

LAB TO LAND

Do *we* know what we are eating? Before we eat anything, we should ask ourselves a simple question: "Did this food come from the lab or from the land?" If we trace the food back to the *lab*oratory, it is probably highly processed and likely contains artificial ingredients, such as flavoring, coloring or dyes, preservatives, and sweeteners, the names of which we can barely pronounce. Our bodies may have a hard time processing these foreign ingredients, which may adversely affect our digestive organs. Foods developed in the lab may also have lower nutrient value per calorie when compared to foods that come to us from the land. Fresh foods from the land, with minimal processing, can help us ward off or manage some ailments.

Each day we should ask ourselves, "What percentage of the foods I ate today was from the lab and what percentage was from the land?" Was it 80 percent lab and

LAB

LAND

only 20 percent land? Perhaps in a move toward greater well-being, we could shift toward 50 percent lab/50 percent land and, eventually, to 20 percent lab/80 percent land. Or perhaps as a starting point, for every lab food we eat, we could eat a food from the land. For every soft drink we consume, we could drink a glass of water, or for every candy bar we consume, we could eat a piece of fruit. While shopping, we could review our basket before we check out and decide not to bring lab products into our home, where we know we will eventually eat them! Over time, our taste buds will return to enjoying foods from the land and our craving for high levels of salt, sugar, fat, and processed foods will decline.

The Greek soul is found in its food; food prepared with love. The rituals of preparing, cooking, sharing, eating, and enjoying food have been passed down through the generations. Simple ingredients are mixed and matched to create unique dishes. The food is cooked slowly to preserve the nutrients, and because olive oil is best when cooked at low temperatures. If the food is boiled in water, the water (and the nutrients that end up in it) is kept to make soup or another meal; it is never just thrown away. Food is eaten slowly and the villagers relax after the meal to give time for proper digestion.

BEANS, GREENS, VEGGIES, AND HERBS

The OPA! Way Lifestyle is focused on a plant-based diet. (We do not include the quantities in the following descriptions of food because every person has unique needs that depend on his or her size, level of activity, and desired health. Eat in proportion to the needs of your body and always consult your doctor before starting any new diet.)

> **Beans:** For simplicity's sake, we've named all the following as beans: legumes, beans, peas, chickpeas (garbanzo), lentils, *gigantes* (big white beans), fava (yellow split peas), pulses, etc. Beans are a miracle food and worshipped highly in the villages of Greece. Unlike fresh fruit and vegetables, which are seasonal, beans are easily stored for winter; bean stew is a common winter staple in the traditional village. Because they are high in protein, beans eaten with whole grains offer an alternative to red meat. They promote heart health and digestive health.

> **Greens:** Greens and vegetables are the main course in Greece. As low-fat, high-nutrient foods, leafy greens can serve an important role in reducing inflammation, which is a cause of heart disease and cancer. Some of the miracle greens in Greece are the following:

> > • Horta are wild greens or grasses, which are gathered from the hillsides throughout the spring, summer, and autumn, or cultivated and sold in farmers markets. They are simply prepared, cooked with olive oil, and served with lemon to offset their bitter taste.

> > • Dandelion leaves are a special type of horta, gathered from the hillsides where no pesticides or herbicides have been used. They are

a rich source of nutrients and also aid in digestion, flushing toxins from the body.

- Grape leaves, commonly known as "dolmades" or "dolmas," are stuffed with rice, herbs, and sometimes meat, and then rolled and cooked. They are a good source of vitamins and fiber.

- Spinach is high in vitamins E and K, along with iron, folate, calcium, protein, and fiber. Some would say it is an antiaging food! Perhaps that's why we find so many variations of spanakopita—baked spinach and feta in phyllo pastry—throughout Greece.

- Purslane is a miracle green because it is high in vitamins C and E and omega-3s. These leafy greens, an alternative to spinach, are steamed or simply put in a salad.

Veggies: Veggies are full of amazing antioxidants and phytochemicals that give us energy and slow the aging process. Vegetables are a good source of protein, provide fiber to aid in digestion, help regulate glucose metabolism, and strengthen our overall immune system. The Greeks in the village eat many more vegetables than fruits during the day. (Their total vegetable and fruit consumption is also far beyond the normal consumption in most other countries.) While iceberg lettuce and potatoes are a favorite green and veggie in America, the Greeks' favorite veggies include the following:

- **Tomatoes:** There is nothing better than a ripe, juicy, deep-red Greek tomato! "It's the sun—that's why our fruits and vegetables taste so wonderful," proudly exclaimed our cousin Elsa. Tomatoes are high in lycopene,

EMBRACE *WELL-BEING*

a powerful antioxidant that reduces inflammation and keeps the blood flowing throughout the body.

- **Eggplant:** This vegetable is abundant throughout Greece and included in many dishes, including moussaka, a layered dish that can contain eggplant, potatoes, ground meat, tomatoes, and cheese. Eggplant is a wonder veggie because it is high in fiber as well as nasunin, a phytonutrient and antioxidant that may help fight aging and cancer.

- **Onions:** Throughout famines and occupations, the Greeks relied on the onion as a staple food. Onions provide powerful antioxidants that fight inflammation and may help with arthritis.

Herbs: For simplicity's sake, we have referred to all herbs and spices as herbs. Tracing back to the sanctuaries dedicated to Asklepios and the work of Hippocrates, herbs have been used to treat wounds, cure illnesses, and restore equilibrium in the body. Many of our pharmaceutical remedies today are derived from ingredients that come originally from plants and herbs. It is said that there are more than five hundred different species native to Greece.

In Greece, herbs are as important as olive oil because, along with their medicinal uses, they are also used to flavor food. In many cases, herbs and spices are used in place of salt, sugar, and heavy cream sauces. Common herbs include oregano, dill, mint, thyme, sage, bay leaves, rosemary, parsley, and basil. Common spices include garlic, cloves, and cinnamon. Of interest, mastic, the resin from mastic trees on the Greek island of Chios, is believed to have multiple therapeutic properties, including as an aid for our teeth and stomachs.

GRAINS AND NUTS

Grains: During a visit to a local bakery in Greece, we discovered that many of the loaves of bread we touched felt hard and stale. We soon realized that what we were touching were Cretan rusks, a type of high-fiber, dry, crispy bread that bounces back to life when it is dipped in olive oil, water, wine, or other liquid. This bread contains no preservatives and is minimally processed. The darker and heavier the bread (usually made with rye, barley, and oat), the healthier it may be.

We discovered many types of breads in Greece with different purposes: everyday breads; breads for certain festival days, such as Easter and Christmas; breads to be used in church services; and special occasion breads adorned with symbols, such as birds and flowers, and used for engagements, weddings, and baptisms. Making these special breads is a community effort, wherein the ladies of the village gather to make hundreds to be presented as gifts for the guests at, for example, a wedding or baptism.

The preferred bread in Greece is whole grain bread, which means literally that the whole grain or all parts of the grain kernel were used, thereby keeping the grain closest to its natural state. This is in stark contrast to more highly processed, bleached breads that are low in nutrients and high in chemicals that are needed to extend shelf life and make it cheaper to produce.

Nuts: Nuts are one of the main snacks in Greece and are often mixed with fruit and cinnamon for dessert. Most of us don't eat enough nuts, which are rich in omega-3 fatty acids (the good kind). Nuts also provide oil that can protect the heart.

FRUIT

"Now we will have dessert," exclaimed cousin Maria as she cleared away the dishes from our main course. "Now we will have fruit." In Greece, traditional dessert rarely consists of sugary baked goods; rather, it consists of fresh fruit, such as grapes, figs, apples, or oranges, and sometimes, Greek yogurt topped with fruit or fruit preserves. We especially enjoy the simple dessert of orange slices sprinkled with cinnamon. Traditionally, Greeks are known to eat three or four times more fruit than what is consumed in most other countries. Some fruits, like pomegranates, even have special status in Greece, as they are believed to bring good luck!

Raw fruit helps with digestion and, because it is slowly absorbed into the bloodstream, does not cause the sugar high and sugar crash like other sugary desserts can do. Besides aiding digestion, fruit can decrease blood pressure and is an excellent source of vitamin C.

Olives are also considered a fruit. A plate of olives is usually offered in every Greek home. Olives are not eaten straight from the tree; they are usually soaked in a salt solution for several weeks to a year. Just as there are many varieties of grapes and wine, there are many varieties of olives (black, green, wrinkled) from different regions in Greece, such as the well-known Kalamata and Koroneiki varieties of Greek olives.

FIVE LIQUIDS OF THE GODS

We've designated the "five liquids of the gods" to be olive oil, honey, lemon, water, and wine.

> **Olive oil:** Ever since Athena gave it as a gift, the Greeks have cultivated the olive tree and used its products for their daily needs. (Homer referred to olive oil as "liquid gold.") The olive is the fruit of the tree and

233

olive oil is the liquid from this fruit. The varying types of olive oil relate to the process of making it: Extra-virgin olive oil comes from the first pressing, is the purest with the best flavor, and has an acidity of less than 0.8 percent. The color of olive oil can vary from green to golden yellow, depending on the type of olive used and how it was harvested and pressed. The terms "light" and "extra light" refer to the color of the oil. Based on what we've learned from trusted Greek olive oil experts, we prefer the dark-green extra-virgin olive oil, which we buy in small quantities and store in a dark, cool place.

Olive oil is an essential ingredient in every Greek kitchen and on every table. The Greeks are world champions in olive oil consumption and it is said that olive oil runs through their veins! Ancel Keys, in his famous "Seven Countries" study (comparing the health of men in Finland, Italy, Greece [Crete], Japan, United States, Yugoslavia, and the Netherlands), found that the Cretan men had the best health, lowest incidence of heart disease, and best longevity, which he attributed to the high consumption of olive oil as the main source of fat in their diet. He noted that the food in Greece basically was swimming in olive oil! Significantly, in the Cretan lifestyle, it is not just the presence of olive oil that contributes to health, but also its role in facilitating the high consumption of vegetables, beans, fish, and grains.

Butter is used sparingly, primarily for baking. Bread is not smothered with butter; it is usually dipped in healthy olive oil.

Honey: References to the production of honey can be traced back to the Minoans in Crete and to the writings of Aristotle. As a natural sweetener, honey, especially dark-colored honey, may be a healthier choice for adult bodies than processed white sugar is, due to its lower glycemic index (meaning it is released more slowly into the bloodstream). Honey contains valuable vitamins and antioxidants and is commonly used as a treatment for sore throats and coughs. The type, flavor, quality, and nutritional value of honey are directly related to the environment in which the bees lived and the type of vegetation the bees visited (for example, fruit, flowers, pine, fir, eucalyptus, thyme, rosemary or sage trees, and other plants). Some of the unspoiled areas of Greece are ideal environments for the production of a wide variety of high quality honey products.

Lemon: Lemon is the wonder fruit of Greece! Lemon is squeezed generously on everything from fish to vegetables to meat dishes, to add zesty flavor, as well as for its health benefits. Lemon and water, sometimes spiced with honey and cinnamon, is a common morning drink used to cleanse the liver and aid in detoxifying the body. High in vitamin C, iron, fiber, calcium, and other elements, lemons are believed to soothe sore throats, lower cholesterol, lower the acid in our digestive tract, delay the absorption of carbohydrates and starches into our stomachs, and help prevent the formation of kidney stones.

Water: Water is critical for helping to maintain hydration and for flushing out toxins. With some people getting up to 20 percent of their daily calories from processed beverages that quickly cause them to put on extra weight, learning to enjoy the simple things in life, like a fresh, clear glass of water, can represent an easy first step in getting healthier.

We've also included tea and coffee in the water section. Tea is a traditional beverage enjoyed in Greece, tracing back to the times of the Minoans and ancient Greeks who used wild herbs for healing. While visiting YiaYia Maria in her village, we were treated to one of her "mountain teas," a special blend of herbs she gathers from the hillside then stores in jars for use throughout the year, especially during winter. These teas are simply boiled in a pot of water for several minutes, strained, and then a squeeze of lemon and a bit of honey are added. Mountain teas are believed to aid in digestion and cleanse the body of toxins, help with respiratory infections and arthritis, soothe aches and pains, as well as provide a sense of calm and general well-being.

Coffee was first imported to Greece around 1500 AD and quickly became an important element of Greek culture. To the Greeks, brewing the perfect cup of coffee is an art form. They have a unique way of preparing their coffee, often using a special pot called a *briki*, in which they boil the water, coffee grounds, and sugar all together. The strong, thick coffee, including the grounds and foam, is served in small cups and is accompanied by an additional glass of water. The custom is to allow the grounds to settle and then sip the coffee very slowly while enjoying the social setting.

Wine: Wine is usually consumed in moderation and with meals, which slows down its absorption. A moderate amount of wine is good for the heart, especially the polyphenols and resveratrol found in red wine that help relax the arteries and keep the blood flowing.

There are many good vintage wines that come from Greece, including those made by Boutari from grapes grown in the volcanic-ash soil in Santorini. There are also good wines that come from the foothills of the White Mountains in Crete, where the warm sea air meets the high mountain air and the wild herbs and nature influence the wines, including those from the Dourakis and Manousakis Wineries. Retsina, a Greek wine infused with the sap of pine trees, is an acquired taste, and one that we have yet to truly acquire!

DAIRY

Because some dairy products are high in fat, acidic, and difficult to digest (since they contain a sugar called lactose), the Greeks in the traditional villages limit their consumption mostly to yogurt and cheese. Some believe that dairy products made from sheep and goat milk are easier to digest than those made from cow milk.

Yogurt is a favorite dairy product: consumed alone, with fruit, and used as an ingredient in a variety of savory dishes. Traditional Greek yogurt is usually thicker than other yogurts and rarely contains any preservatives or sugars. It is an excellent source of protein, calcium, vitamin B6, and vitamin B12. Greek yogurt is particularly good for the digestive system as its live microorganisms help with digestion, boost the metabolism, and lower the chance of infection.

Feta is the most well-known cheese from Greece and has recently been awarded a special status in the European Union: PDO or "Protected Designation of Origin," meaning that legally Feta cheese can only be produced in Greece and must be produced using the traditional methods. Traditional Feta is made from sheep or goat's milk, not from cow's milk. In general, cheese is used sparingly in Greek cooking, unlike in some other countries where it has become a main ingredient.

FISH

In many locations in Greece, the meal can simply swim to the table! Surrounded by its crystal blue waters, Greece is blessed with an abundance of life energy from the sea. The sight of the octopus (a word with Greek roots that literally means "eight feet") being pounded against the rocks and then hung to dry outside the taverna, shows the Greeks reliance on the sea. Fish (seafood) is an important component of their healthy diet. Fish is rich in omega-3 fatty acids, which help thin the blood and keep it flowing. Fish oil is also believed to be good for fighting depression as well as for improving mental functions.

In Greece, it's also interesting to see that the fish and other foods from the sea are prepared simply—with olive oil, a few local herbs, and of course, a squirt of lemon. It would seem almost sacrilegious for Greeks to smother or layer fish with high-fat cream sauces.

SWEETS, TREATS, AND MEATS

Sweets and Treats: Greeks are famous for their baked sweets, including baklava (honey and nuts between sheets of phyllo pastry), *melomakarona* (honey-soaked cookies), *koulourakia* (twisted, biscotto-like cookies), as well as rice pudding and spoon sweets, which are made with natural sweeteners like honey and grape juice syrup. Unlike those in North America who eat sweets and treats every day, most Greeks save these sweets for very special occasions. The Greeks in the village would be shocked at the variety and amount of candy and snacks (made with sugar and artificial chemicals) we consume every day.

Meats: Greeks are famous for their meat dishes, especially souvlaki (small pieces of meat grilled on a skewer), and the gyro (meat roasted on a vertical spit that is usually served in a pita bread sandwich). One of our cousins explained to us that the animals in Greece are very healthy since they eat healthy plants and drink fresh water as they wander around the hillsides.

Traditionally in Greece, meat was a special occasion food and was not eaten regularly due to its limited availability and high cost. Over time, meat gained a reputation for being part of a "rich man's diet," and plants (greens, vegetables, and beans) were associated with a "poor man's diet." Meat has also become a meaningful symbol of celebration and hospitality: "We might not be wealthy, but we will honor your presence by offering you some meat." And, of course, when such a special occasion for celebration and hospitality arises and you are offered meat, you cannot refuse for fear of insulting your host!

In North America, we typically fill our plates with meat and then add a few side dishes, such as potatoes and cooked vegetables. Whereas in Greece, plates are typically filled with greens and grains first and then, only occasionally, is some fish, chicken, or red meat added. Because of the fasting calendar, red meat might only be eaten twice a month. Besides fish, their alternative sources for protein are beans (such as lentils), grains (oatmeal, barley, and rye), vegetables (tomatoes, spinach, eggplant, and broccoli), fruits, and nuts.

Summary

Greece could lead the world in teaching a holistic approach to well-being. Taking good care of spirit, mind, and body is ingrained in the culture. Greeks know that life is about energy, and well-being is about keeping this important life energy flowing. We can all adopt the Hippocratic Oath, "do no harm," by replacing excessive stress, overeating, eating poor quality foods, and inactivity, with healthier choices. We can all adopt The OPA! Way Lifestyle, which integrates the practices of moderation, movement, outdoors, rejuvenation, and good nutrition. We can all revisit our relationship with food and begin to eat more like *yiayia* eats—more land, less lab! Adopting one thing a day from The OPA! Way Lifestyle pyramid is a good place to start.

All of us have the capacity to find joy and meaning in our life and work. By appreciating the *fullness of life*, by living confidently and fearlessly (*aphobia*) and by adopting the habits of *well-being*, we can all embrace life with attitude. In doing so, we discover that we matter, that we are part of something special, and that our lives do, indeed, have meaning. OPA!

OPA! AFFIRMATION

I find joy and meaning in my life when I embrace life with well-being.

(Again, as with any health-related information, please consult your physician to discuss your personal situation.)

Part Five

The Odyssey Continues . . .

12

Everybody Say "OPA!"

"OPA! Day." That's what we called the special day we invented, on which people around the world can celebrate Greek culture and the many contributions Greeks have made throughout the ages in such areas as: astronomy, architecture, art, biology, democracy, drama, food and diet, language, literature, mathematics, medicine, music, philosophy, politics, psychology, science, sports, and theater. Of course, we also celebrate, in the spirit of The OPA! Way, the wisdom on how to live and work with meaning. We chose September 15 as OPA! Day since it also just happens to be the United Nations International Day of Democracy. It was also extremely important to us to hold the first OPA! Day celebration in Greece.

It was an exceptionally sunny day and the sea appeared bluer than ever. More than four hundred Greeks and visitors from around the world gathered to attend the very first OPA! Day event, on September 15, 2010, in beautiful and historic Rethymno, Crete. Our partners at the lovely and truly hospitable Aegean Pearl Hotel prepared an extraordinary celebration—with beautiful blue and white decorations, tables full of traditional Greek and Cretan mezes, and newly invented OPA! Day drinks.

The event, which was covered extensively by both the Greek print and electronic media, included presentations about the meaning and significance of OPA! Day; the proclamation of OPA! Day by the mayor of Rethymno, followed by the cutting of a specially made OPA! Day cake; with mingling among the international guests and dignitaries, connecting meaningfully with one another around the delicious Greek food; and the enjoyment of traditional Greek music, with dancing well into the night. And, of course, everyone remembered to wear something blue, a national color of Greece.

Besides now being an official holiday in Rethymno, its recognized "birthplace," OPA! Day has also been celebrated on five continents since 2010, with more sites around the world joining the celebration every year! Moreover, in 2012, the City of Santa Fe, New Mexico, became the first in North America to officially recognize the day by approving a resolution naming September 15 "OPA! Day" and, for the first time, OPA! Day was also celebrated in the People's Republic of China.

The birth of OPA! Day in 2010 marked the beginning of the global initiative to celebrate all things Greek. We invite you to celebrate OPA! Day each year, on September 15, in your community, town, city, state, or province. Celebrate Greek culture in restaurants, tavernas, bars, stores, schools, colleges, universities, and city centers. Celebrate with Greek food, drinks, dancing, and, of course, by wearing something blue! Unleash your "inner Greek" and join us in the OPA! Movement! The world can always use a little more OPA!

As we return to the meaning-focused question that began our odyssey through Greece, we realize that, in many ways, we are coming full circle back to the question the ancient Greek philosophers asked thousands of years ago: "How do we live the good life?" Or, as we interpret it, "How do we live the meaningful life?" On many levels, we realize that Greece is more a state of mind than it is a location. Upon further reflection, we realize that meaning is a common thread that runs through all cultures. Meaning, in other words, is at the heart and spirit of what makes us human.

OPA! Insights

The OPA! Way, in effect, is a new story inclusive of the past, present, and future. It is a new paradigm to help us understand ourselves and our world. It teaches us that meaning is found in the integration of others (O), purpose (P), and attitude (A). All of the core lessons in The OPA! Way are interrelated and interdependent, just as the areas of our lives are interrelated and interdependent, and just as spirit, mind, and body are interrelated and interdependent. Struggles or changes in one area of life—either at home or at work—affect the other areas.

To reinforce the core lessons we've shared through our journey and in this book, we've included important highlights for you to review and remember as you follow your own path to living and working with meaning:

Others (O)

> **Connect with *The Village*:** The Greeks taught us that no one and nothing can exist in isolation. We are all important participants in the different "villages" in our lives. Importantly, a village divided lacks strength; however, a united village has both strength and energy.

> **Connect with *Hospitality*:** Meaning can be found in the simplicity of extending hospitality to others and in appreciating and being grateful for all acts of kindness, no matter how small.

Connect with *Honor*: We can connect more meaningfully with others by seeing ourselves in others and respecting them. We can show honor by treating others as we wish to be treated because "what goes around eventually comes around."

Purpose (P)

Engage with *"Know Thyself"*: Along our journey of self-discovery, we need to ask deep questions to know who we really are and to recognize how far we may have drifted from our authentic selves. The Greeks taught us to always act in accordance with our true nature.

Engage with *Arete*: In a world full of change, the Greeks taught us to engage with our arete, our virtues and core values, so that we can make the best choices for ourselves and others.

Engage with *Evdemonia*: The Greeks taught us to stop chasing happiness and start looking for meaning. The end goal of life is evdemonia, a concept involving deep fulfillment, inner and outer prosperity, and being of service to others.

Attitude (A)

Embrace *The Fullness of Life*: The Greeks taught us that life is short and ever-changing. They taught us to embrace the fullness of life, all the ups and downs, the joys and sorrows, with zest and an appreciation for being alive.

Embrace *Aphobia*: We can always choose how to see the world—we can see scarcity or we can see abundance. We can retreat in fear or we can move forward, through the fear. With every event or situation that unfolds in our lives, we always have the freedom to choose how we respond.

Embrace *Well-Being***:** Life is about energy and it is important that we use our energy wisely. Stress and an unhealthy lifestyle can drain our energy. The OPA! Way lifestyle is a new and very unique paradigm that integrates others, purpose, and attitude with daily practices of rejuvenation, movement, and proper nutrition.

In Closing

The real crisis in the global economy is the Crisis of Meaning. The real crisis behind our dissatisfaction, stress, and unhealthy lifestyles is the Crisis of Meaning. The real crisis behind employee disengagement and other work-related issues is the Crisis of Meaning.

In times of crisis, when we are struggling or lacking fulfillment, we need to go back to the basics in life and search for the sources of true meaning. Meaning is all around us, waiting to be discovered. Because meaning is not only the fuel that drives us toward our goals in life but also is the primary link to our core essence, it is imperative that we make the search for meaning a priority in our lives.

It is not the search for the meaning of life that is important; rather, it is the search for meaning *in your own life* that is most important. Meaning is different for everyone—there is no one right answer—there is only the answer that is *right* for you.

As we begin to understand what is meaningful—what really matters to us—we begin to transform and enter the process of becoming who we are really meant to be. When we understand and act from our own Core of Meaning, we become more engaged and resilient, more energetic and healthy, more creative and productive. We truly live and work with meaning.

As Heraclitus taught us, the sun is new each day. Each day is a new opportunity to look for and discover joy and meaning in our lives. Each day opens up new opportunities to learn, live, work, practice, and share The OPA! Way approach to living and working with joy and meaning. At the end of each day and at the end of our lives, there are really only two questions we need to ask ourselves: "Did I find meaning?" and "Did I help others find meaning?"

OPA!

OPA! AFFIRMATION

*I find joy and meaning in my life when I live and work
The OPA! Way.*

Acknowledgments

In the words of one of our friends in Greece, *The OPA! Way* is our "literal return to Ithaka" for it represents, along the lines of Homer in his epic poem *The Odyssey*, our account of a long journey during which we had many adventures and challenges, as well as met many people along the way. And like Odysseus, we necessarily relied upon help from others, be it for their service, guidance, and moral support. Indeed, without their help, we may never have reached the shore and completed our meaning-focused mission successfully. As destiny would have it, these individuals proved to be our gods and goddesses in disguise, always showing up when we needed them the most. To each and every one of you, including those who are Greek, those of Greek heritage, and friends of Greece (Philhellenes), we are forever grateful for, and will always honor, your presence on the path toward completing this book.

Against this backdrop, we'd like to recognize our fellow argonauts from the United States, Canada, Greece, and around the world.

In the United States, we were privileged to receive ongoing encouragement and heartfelt support from leaders representing many of the nation's most prominent Greek/Hellenic organizations, including: Arthur Dimopoulos, Tony Gianoulis, Nick Larigakis, Basil Mossaides, Gregory C. Pappas, George A. Passes, and Emmanuel E. Velivasakis. On an individual level, we are very proud of our meaningful connection to members of the Greek American community: Andreas Akaras, John Aniston, John P. Calamos Sr., Mari Carras, Alexander Christakis, Eleni Daniels, Yanna Darilis, Alki David, Antonis H. Diamataris, George Dratelis, Michael Dukakis, Chrysoula Economopoulos,

Vasile G. Faklis, Nikos Gaitatjis, Archelle Georgiou, Rick Hercules, Maria Hnaraki, Arianna Huffington, Maria Fotinopoulos Karamitsos, Anthoula Katsimatides, Nymphe Kefal, Asenath Kepler, Panos Kinigakis, Paul Kotrotsios, Robert Krantz, Evan Lambrou, Niki Leondakis, Helene Liatsos, Emilie Litsas, Nick Maniatis, Adonis Maropis, Debbie Matenopoulos, Eric Metaxas, John Metaxas, Connie Mourtoupalas, Michael Nevradakis, Peter Nikkos, Shelly Papadopoulos, Fr. Dimitrios Pappas, Renee Pappas, Mary Papoulias-Platis, Terry Poulos, Leonardo Razatos, Brenda Ropoulos, Christine Salboudis, John Sarbanes, Ramsay Seikaly, Yannis Simonides, Constantine Sirigos, Agapi Stassinopoulos, George E. Stephanopoulos, Terry Stratoudakis, Kerry Tramontanas, Katina Vaselopulos, E. Mike Vasilomanolakis, Frederika Vaupen, and Frank Yiannas.

We are also grateful for the interest in and support of The OPA! Way paradigm and lifestyle, including our new book, that we received from many American Philhellenes, including: Larry Ahrens, Arthur Arndt, Joseph Badal, Meridee Barker, Karen Bloom, Ed and Eva Borins, Jon Bowman, Peter Capozzi, Linda Carfagno, Mary Cimiluca, David Coss, Barbara Crook, Joseph Coughlin, Anna Darrah, Paul DeDomenico, Larry and Barbara Dossey, Keri Douglas, Brit Elders, Irene Estrada, Don Fertman, Michelle Gielan, Steven Kampmann, Debbie Kennedy, Daniela Kestelman, Alana Elias Kornfeld, George Kruft, Raymond Kurshals, Robert Lavigna, Jerome Lewis, George R. R. Martin, Jennifer Martin, W. Scott Matthews, Merritt Mecham, Greg Menke, Jeff Pasternak, Bryce Perrin, Michele Rosenthal, Jay Shanker, Michael Skaggs, Sandra Staggs, Matt Townsend, Nguyen Anh Tuan, William Van Eron, Johnny Vollersten, and Rebecca Wurzburger.

A number of family members in the United States deserve mention for standing by us through thick and thin, even when our ship appeared to go off course due to unexpected winds: Arion and Maria Pattakos, George and Helen Pattakos, Gregory T. Pattakos, and Cornelia Pattakos Pinney.

Farther north, in Canada, we also were blessed with support from both the Greek Canadian community and friends of Greece. In the former group, we would like to call out the support of Aggy Apostolopoulos, Andonis Artemakis, Georgia Balogiannis, George Gekas, Nick Georgakopoulos, Greg Kanargelidis, Debbie Papadakis, Michael Papamarkakis, and Thomas S. Saras; in the latter, we would also like to thank Gabe Amatruda, Carolyn Bennett, Sandy French, Corina Gottschling and Dave Stevenson, Les Hine, Peter Jones, Daniel Jordan, Kesa Matson, Dennis Mills, and Brenda Wood for being such wonderful and loyal partners on the road.

The OPA! Way is grounded firmly in the soil and soul of Greece. In this connection, we are indebted to the many Greek citizens who influenced our thinking, encouraged us to pursue our quest, engaged us in authentic Greek experiences, and guided us safely along our odyssey in Greece. A case in point is our close relationship with a number of key people in Rethymno, Crete, Greece, the birthplace of OPA! Day: Eugenios Fragiadakis, Yiannis Katsoulis, and George Shoinas of the Aegean Pearl Hotel; Mayor George Marinakis; Pepi Birliraki-Mamalaki, vice-mayor and city councillor, with responsibility for Culture and Tourism; and Professor Kostas A. Lavdas, University of Crete. Our extensive Cretan connections also include many colleagues and dear friends who are now part of our extended family: Koula Barydakis, Antonis Dourakis, Yiorgos Hadjidakis, Antonis Lambrinos, Matheos Marketakis, Lambros Papoutsakis, Peter Parasirakis, Sifis Plimakis, Manos Sfyrakis, Argiro Stavrakaki, Marianna Founti-Vassi, and Christina Zografaki.

And speaking of family, we are extremely thankful for the love and support that we've received from our many

Greek relatives, including: Aimilia Kapetanaki, Antonis and Maria Pattakos, Alexandros A. and Maria Pattakos, Giorgos I. Pattakos, Gina Pattakos, Iakovos Pattakos and Elsa Kakogiannaki Pattakos, Persefoni Pattakos, Stylianos Pattakos, Yannis Prokopakis and Argiro Petraki, Diogenis and Vicky Stavroulakis, and Thanasis Stavroulakis.

We also learned and experienced much from other members of our extended Greek "framily": Alkistis Agiorgiti, Sofia Tsakiroglou-Bothou, Konstantinos Bouas, Andy Dabilis, George Economides, Peter Economides, Patricia Kara, Chrysoula Karametros, Panagiotis Karkatsoulis, Petros Katsimardos, Sylvia Klimaki, Diane Kochilas, Kyriakos Kyriakakis, Constantine Krystallis, Margarita Manousou, Aliki Mitsakos, Sophia Economou-Nikiforakis, Ariadne Nowak, Zoe Nowak, Kostas Panagiotopoulos, Nikos Skoulas, Alex Stefanopoulos, Efi Stefopoulou, Roula Tsikiroglou-Tsalavoutas, Periklis Tsiagkouris, Efthimios Tsiliopoulos, Foteini Varela, and Dimitris Yannopoulos.

On a more global basis, we also must recognize the kind support for The OPA! Way that we received from both people of Greek heritage and friends of Greece around the world, especially: Steve Agi (Australia), Dirk Dalichau (Hong Kong), Andreas Deffner (Germany), Claudio Drapkin and Nuria Povill (Spain), Bess Hepworth (Hong Kong), Yianna Kirkwood (South Africa), Charlotte Lavender (United Kingdom), Evangelos Louizidis (China), Maria Ines Palumbo (Italy), Angelos Pangratis (Switzerland), and Lesley Rogers (Tasmania). And we would be remiss if we didn't acknowledge the thousands of other supporters from around the world who, individually and collectively, have helped to bring The OPA! Way into everyday life and work.

As authors, we are indebted to our literary agent extraordinaire, William Gladstone, founder of Waterside Productions, for believing in us and what we were seeking

ACKNOWLEDGMENTS

to do with *The OPA! Way* and, importantly, for supporting Greece in her time of need by helping us to make this book a reality. Likewise, we would like to thank Waterside's Neil Gudovitz, head of its foreign rights division, for his authentic commitment to advancing this book, *The OPA! Way*, in global markets.

Of course, this book wouldn't exist if it weren't for the decision by our publisher, BenBella Books, to take it on! For this decision, we must thank Glenn Yeffeth and his extraordinary team at BenBella for hearing our call for meaning and for unleashing their "inner Greek" by embracing The OPA! Way paradigm in concept and practice. In addition to Glenn, we are honored to have had the opportunity to sail the open seas during our odyssey with the following BenBella argonauts: Heather Butterfield, Jennifer Canzoneri, Sarah Dombrowsky, Alicia Kania, Adrienne Lang, Monica Lowry, Lindsay Marshall, Cameron Proffitt, Jessika Rieck, Jenna Sampson, and Leah Wilson. Thank you all for sharing your extraordinary talents and for helping to keep us on course!

Finally, Alex would like to pay tribute to his late father, Nicholas G. Pattakos, a proud Greek American of Cretan heritage, whose inspiration and memory will be eternal, and who instilled in Alex the true Greek spirit. And to our dog, Bouvie, who is no longer with us on a physical plane but is always with us in spirit: We thank you for your unconditional love, your inspiration, and your everlasting influence on living and working with joy and meaning. OPA!

Join the OPA! Movement!

Visit our website: www.theopaway.com

Join the online OPA! Village

Take the OPA! Meaning Tests

Sign up for our monthly "Everybody Say OPA!" eblast

Follow us on Twitter: @TheOPAWay

"Like" us on Facebook: www.facebook.com/ TheOPAWay

Start a book discussion group about *The OPA! Way*

Attend OPA! workshops and retreats

Become a certified OPA! Associate

Bring The OPA! Way into your organization and workplace

Celebrate OPA! Day every September 15

Live and work The OPA! Way

About the Authors

ALEX PATTAKOS. A proud Greek-American (of Cretan heritage), Alex Pattakos, PhD, cofounder of The Meaning Group, has been described as a modern-day Greek philosopher. Also affectionately nicknamed "Dr. Meaning," he is focused on bringing meaning to work, the workplace, and into everyday life. He is the author of the international best-selling book *Prisoners of Our Thoughts*, which is available in twenty-two languages and based on the wisdom of his mentor, the world-renowned psychiatrist Dr. Viktor Frankl, who personally urged him to write it. A U.S. Army veteran with expertise in political science and psychology, Dr. Pattakos has been privileged to work internationally with all levels of government, including service to three presidential administrations in the White House. Dr. Pattakos is a former therapist and mental health administrator, as well as a political campaign organizer, community- and economic-development policy planner, and full-time professor of public and business administration.

Dr. Pattakos was one of the initial faculty evaluators for the Innovations in American Government Awards Program at the John F. Kennedy School of Government, Harvard University, and a past president of Renaissance Business Associates (RBA), an international nonprofit association of people committed to elevating the human spirit in the workplace. During his tenure as president, RBA was active in Australia, Canada, Europe, Nigeria, South Africa, and the United States. Dr. Pattakos is a member of the International Academic Board; The International Center for Leading Studies, Athens, Greece; and the Board of Thinkers, Boston Global Forum.

ELAINE DUNDON. Elaine Dundon, co-founder and CEO of The Meaning Group, began her career in business strategy and marketing, including brand management at Procter & Gamble, Nestle, and Kraft Foods. A thought leader in the field of innovation management, she  authored the international best-selling book *The Seeds of Innovation*, as well as created and taught the groundbreaking course on Innovation Management for the business program at the University of Toronto, Canada. Her work in the field of innovation has been featured globally in numerous leading publications. Dundon has worked with and advised some of the world's best businesses, government agencies, and nonprofit organizations, including ADP, American Society for Quality, AstraZeneca, Cargill, Carlson Hotels Worldwide, Citigroup, The Conference Board of Canada, Four Seasons Hotels and Resorts, Heart and Stroke Foundation, Mars, the Mayo Clinic, Ontario Public Service (Canada), PricewaterhouseCoopers, Civil Service College Singapore, and Vancity, among others.

As her work in innovation management evolved, Dundon's focus shifted to the "human side of innovation," and, specifically, meaning, which her experience and research have shown is the key source of success. To augment her research, Dundon often traveled to Greece and studied metaphysics and Greek philosophy. Now as a meaning strategist, keynote speaker, advisor, and facilitator, she is leading the Meaning Movement by encouraging leaders to inspire meaningful engagement and innovation as well as encouraging all to live and work The OPA! Way.

For Further Information:
Email: info@theopaway.com or info@themeaninggroup.com
Web: www.theopaway.com and www.themeaninggroup.com